Fallen Angels and Grey Skies

Fallen Angels and Grey Skies

Aliens, Chemtrails, and the War for Humanity

By Drew Allen

Fallen Angels and Grey Skies - Aliens, Chemtrails, and the War for Humanity

ISBN: 979-8-9934737-0-3 (eBook/Electronic Media)
ISBN: 979-8-9934737-1-0 (Paperback)
ISBN: 979-8-9938072-5-6 (Hardcover)

First Edition (Edited)
Printed in the United States of America

Cover design by Drew Allen
Interior design by Drew Allen

Published by Drew Allen

Preface

This book began with a simple but unsettling question: Why does history feel incomplete?

From the earliest myths to the most modern anomalies, there are patterns of erasure, corruption, and control. Civilizations rise and fall, archives burn, populations are displaced, and yet the same motifs return: forbidden knowledge, hybrid beings, resets by fire and flood, and systems of control that replace covenant with compliance.

The biblical record hints at this: the serpent in Eden, the Watchers on Mount Hermon, the Nephilim before the Flood, the scattering at Babel. Extra-biblical texts like 1 Enoch expand the picture, describing angels who descended, swore oaths, and taught forbidden arts... metallurgy, enchantments, writing, and genetic corruption. Archaeology, folklore, and modern testimony echo these themes: underground halls, anomalous craters, abduction accounts, and ambiguous beings who blur the line between spirit and flesh.

This book is not fiction. It is a synthesis of scripture, folklore, archaeology, comparative mythology, and modern anomalies, woven into a narrative that is imaginative and defensible. Every chapter is anchored in verifiable sources... biblical texts, scholarly works, archaeological reports, and documented historical events. Where speculation enters, it is clearly marked, and always tethered to evidence.

The purpose of this book is not despair, but remembrance. For if the serpent's oldest tactic is to sever humanity from memory, then the antidote is for humanity to remember. To remember covenant. To remember truth. To remember that while hidden forces of corruption persist, so too do hidden forces of preservation that are aligned with GOD.

This book is written for those who sense that history is deeper than textbooks admit, that myth is not mere fantasy, and that the battle between covenant and control is not ancient alone, but ongoing.

May this book serve you as both a warning and a hope: a warning of the systems that seek to erase, and a hope that remembrance, covenant, and the hidden hand of GOD will forever endure.

— Drew Allen

Table of Contents

Introduction

History is not a straight line. It is a manuscript that has been written, erased, and written over again and again. Beneath the surface of every empire, every archive, every monument, there are traces of older stories, older systems, older battles. What we call "progress" often conceals resets. What we call "myth" often preserves memory.

This book is about those hidden layers. It is about the serpent's whisper in Eden, the Watchers' descent on Hermon, the Kenites' stewardship of forbidden knowledge, and the resets of fire, flood, and war that have shaped civilizations. It is about the strange continuity between ancient giants and modern anomalies, between subterranean halls and digital cages, between the corruption of flesh in Genesis and the genetic manipulations of today.

But it is also about something more. It is about remembrance. For if the serpent's oldest tactic is to sever humanity from its memory, then the antidote is to remember. To remember covenant. To remember truth. To remember that the battle is not only ancient but ongoing ... and that it is not one-sided.

Throughout history, hidden forces of corruption have worked to erase, but hidden forces of preservation have worked to restore. Angels, prophets, scribes, reformers, and ordinary men and women have carried memory across the ages. Even now, in an era of digital surveillance and biological engineering, there are faithful forces aligned with GOD who resist, preserve, and remind.

This book does not ask you to accept every claim. It asks you to look again. To see the patterns. To test the sources. To weigh the evidence. And above all, to remember.

For the story of humanity is not only the story of rebellion and control. It is also the story of covenant and hope. And the final word does not belong to the serpent, nor to the Watchers, nor to the systems of control. The final word belongs to the Light that shines in darkness... and is not overcome.

Chapter 1 –
The Serpent's Legacy

"The serpent was the first to whisper knowledge into the ear of man."
— *Mesopotamian proverb (Sumerian fragments)*

The serpent in Eden was more than a tempter; it was the archetype of estrangement. Genesis 3 records the first corruption of covenant: the whisper that humanity could be "as gods" by severing dependence on GOD. This was not brute force but subtle manipulation… the replacement of remembrance with doubt. The serpent's legacy is not merely sin… it is the pattern of control through deception. From this moment, the battle lines were drawn: covenant versus estrangement, remembrance versus erasure, freedom versus control.

The Serpent

The serpent in Eden was not merely a creature of temptation. It was the first architect of estrangement... a being whose subtlety introduced the possibility of rebellion not through force, but through suggestion. In Genesis 3, the serpent's words are precise and calculated: "Ye shall not surely die... ye shall be as gods, knowing good and evil." This was not a lie in the crude sense, but a distortion... a reframing of divine boundaries as limitations to be overcome.

The serpent's legacy begins here: not with violence, but with ambiguity. It did not destroy the covenant; it undermined it. It did not deny GOD's word; it reinterpreted it. And in doing so, it introduced a devious new system... one based not on remembrance, but on autonomy, knowledge divorced from relationship, and power severed from purpose.

This moment marks the first fracture in the human story. Eve's decision, followed by Adam's, was not merely disobedience... it was a shift in allegiance. The tree of knowledge was not forbidden because knowledge itself was evil, but because it represented a form of knowing apart from GOD. The serpent offered gnosis without covenant, enlightenment without obedience, and selfhood without submission.

From this fracture, a pattern emerges... one that will echo through every age. The serpent's legacy is not confined to Eden. It reappears in Cain's rebellion, in the descent of the Watchers, in the rise of civilizations estranged from GOD, and in the systems of control that replace covenant with compliance.

The Knowledge of the Serpent

Ancient traditions (biblical, apocryphal, and mythological) suggest that the serpent possessed knowledge beyond that of ordinary beasts. In 1 Enoch, the Watchers teach forbidden arts: metallurgy, enchantments, writing, and genetic manipulation. The fallen angel Azazel, in particular, is associated with the corruption of flesh and the beautification of war. These teachings mirror the serpent's original tactic: offering knowledge that empowers but estranges from GOD.

In Gnostic texts, the serpent is sometimes reimagined as a liberator... a bringer of enlightenment against a tyrannical creator. Heretical to orthodox theology, this inversion reveals the enduring ambiguity of the serpent archetype. It is a being that blurs categories: divine and demonic, wise and wicked, liberator and deceiver.

The serpent's knowledge is not neutral. It is weaponized. It is used to build systems that appear beneficial but ultimately enslave. From ancient Babylon to modern technocracies, the pattern persists: knowledge becomes control, and control becomes estrangement.

Cain and Abel: A Divided Lineage

Genesis 4 introduces the first murder... Cain slaying Abel. But deeper traditions suggest a more complex origin. Some ancient commentaries, including certain strands of Jewish mysticism and early Christian speculation, propose that Cain and Abel may have had different spiritual lineages. Cain, marked and exiled, becomes a builder of cities and a progenitor of estranged civilization. Abel, the shepherd, represents covenantal innocence.

Whether literal or symbolic, this duality reflects a deeper truth: from the beginning, humanity has been divided between remembrance and rebellion. Cain's descendants, the Kenites, become smiths and scribes, essential to civilization but often estranged from covenant. Abel's line, through Seth, preserves the memory of GOD.

This division is not merely familial; it is archetypal. It echoes in every age, in every system, in every choice between covenant and control.

The Serpent Archetype Across Cultures

The serpent appears in nearly every mythological system:
- In Mesopotamia, it is entwined with the Tree of Life in the Epic of Gilgamesh.
- In Egypt, the uraeus serpent crowns the pharaoh, symbolizing divine authority.
- In Mesoamerica, Quetzalcoatl... the feathered serpent... brings civilization and law.
- In Hindu tradition, the naga are semi-divine serpents who dwell underground and guard sacred knowledge.
- In Norse myth, Jörmungandr encircles the world, destined to rise during Ragnarök.

These serpent beings are often associated with wisdom, thresholds, and transformation... but also with danger, deception, and destruction. They are liminal creatures, dwelling between worlds, offering knowledge that comes with a price.

The Legacy of Estrangement

The serpent's legacy is not a single event, but a system... a way of being that replaces covenant with control, remembrance with manipulation, and divine order with autonomous power. It is the foundation of every empire that rises without GOD, every archive that burns truth, every technology that severs flesh from spirit.

And yet, even here, the antidote remains. For every whisper of estrangement, there is a call to remembrance. For every counterfeit, there is a covenant. For every distortion, there is a truth that endures.

This book begins with the serpent not to glorify it, but to expose it. To trace its legacy through history, myth, and modernity. And to remind the reader that the battle is not over... but neither is it lost.

Chapter 2 –
The First Erasure

"The gods resolved to send a flood to destroy mankind."
— *Epic of Gilgamesh, Tablet XI*

Before the Flood, Genesis 6:12 declares: "All flesh had corrupted his way upon the earth." The corruption was not only moral but biological. The Watchers (fallen angels) descended, took wives, and produced the Nephilim. Civilization advanced, but covenant was forgotten. The Flood was not only a judgment, it was a reset... an erasure of corrupted flesh, a cleansing of memory, a restart of covenant through Noah.

Estrangement

The serpent's whisper in Eden introduced estrangement with GOD. But it was in the generations that followed... through Cain's line, through the Watchers, through the corruption of flesh... and the estrangement became systemic. Genesis 6 records a moment of total saturation: "All flesh had corrupted his way." This was not merely moral decay. It was biological, spiritual, and civilizational. It was a corruption so complete that only erasure could preserve GOD's covenant.

This chapter explores the first global reset (the Flood) not as a myth, but as a strategic judgment. It was the first divine intervention to halt a system of control that had metastasized across the earth.

The Descent of the Watchers

According to 1 Enoch, a group of two hundred fallen angels (Watchers) descended upon Mount Hermon and swore an oath to take human wives. These were not passive observers; they were active corrupters.

Each taught forbidden arts:
- Azazel taught metallurgy and weaponry.
- Semjaza taught enchantments and sorcery.
- Penemue taught writing and manipulation of language.
- Others taught astrology, herbology, and genetic tampering.

Their offspring (the Nephilim) were giants, hybrids, and tyrants. They devoured the earth's resources, enslaved populations, and introduced technologies that accelerated corruption. The Watchers' descent was not enlightenment; it was invasion.

The Corruption of Flesh

Genesis 6:2–4 describes the "sons of GOD" taking wives from the "daughters of men." The resulting offspring were "mighty men of old, men of renown." But their fame masked their corruption. The Hebrew phrase kol basar ("all flesh") implies that the corruption extended beyond humanity. Animals, plants, and ecosystems were affected. The genetic tampering of the Watchers disrupted the created order.

This was not evolution. It was intrusion. The Watchers introduced a counterfeit creation... one that mimicked divine design but severed it from divine purpose.

The Flood as Reset

The Flood was not merely punishment. It was a reset, a strategic erasure of corrupted systems. Noah was chosen not only for righteousness but for purity. Genesis 6:9 describes him as "perfect in his generations," a phrase that some interpret as genetic integrity. His family represented a remnant of uncorrupted flesh.

The ark was not just a vessel of survival. It was a container of memory... preserving covenantal lineage, clean animals, and the possibility of restoration. The Flood erased the corrupted world but preserved the blueprint of divine order.

Post-Flood Remnants

The Flood did not eliminate all threats. The bodies of the Nephilim perished, but their spirits remained. These became the demons of later ages... bodiless, restless, and hungry. The Watchers themselves were supposedly bound in Tartarus, according to 1 Enoch and 2 Peter 2:4, but their influence endured through secret traditions, subterranean refuges, and corrupted bloodlines.

Cain's descendants (the Kenites) reappear after the Flood, suggesting that some lineages survived. Whether through hybrid vessels, underground cities, or spiritual possession, the system of estrangement adapted and endured.

The Pattern of Erasure

The Flood established a pattern: when corruption reaches saturation, then erasure follows. This pattern recurs in later resets such as Babel, Sodom, Egypt, Babylon, Rome. Each time, God intervenes to preserve covenant and memory. Each time, the system of control regroups and reemerges.

The first erasure was global. It was a warning and a precedent. It reminds us that divine patience has limits, and that preservation sometimes requires destruction.

Chapter 3 –
The Kenite Bloodline

"The smith is the master of fire, and fire is the master of men."
— Mircea Eliade, The Forge and the Crucible

Cain's descendants pioneered civilization: metallurgy, music, ornamentation. Yet their innovations were estranged from God. The Kenites, descendants of Cain, appear throughout Scripture as smiths and scribes, indispensable yet never fully integrated into Israel. They represent civilization without covenant, knowledge without wisdom, power without God. Their archetype persists: the outsider who shapes systems through tools and texts.

The Flood Erased Much

The Flood erased much, but not all. Certain lineages, traditions, and fragments of forbidden knowledge survived. Among the most enigmatic of these were the Kenites, a people whose name is derived from Qayin (Cain). Their presence in the biblical record is subtle, yet persistent, and their role in the transmission of knowledge is profound.

The Kenites appear as wanderers, smiths, scribes, and allies of Israel, yet always at the margins. They are both insiders and outsiders, both preservers of memory and stewards of estrangement. To understand their role is to understand how forbidden knowledge survived the first erasure and re-entered the stream of history.

The Origins of the Kenites

The Kenites are first mentioned in Genesis 15:19 as one of the peoples inhabiting the land promised to Abraham. Later, in Numbers 24:21, Balaam describes them as dwelling securely in the rocks. Judges 1:16 records that the descendants of Moses' father-in-law, Jethro the Midianite priest, were Kenites who traveled with Israel into Canaan.

This dual identity, both kin to Israel and yet distinct, is central to their mystery. They are linked to Cain by name, suggesting a lineage that survived the Flood, whether through intermarriage, cultural transmission, or subterranean preservation of knowledge. They are also linked to Midian, a land associated with priesthood and esoteric wisdom.

The Kenites as Smiths and Scribes

The Kenites are associated with metallurgy and writing, two of the forbidden arts taught by the Watchers in 1 Enoch. Tubal-Cain, a descendant of Cain, is described in Genesis 4:22 as "an instructor of every artificer in brass and iron." This tradition of smithing, passed through the Kenites, made them indispensable to ancient societies.

Metallurgy was not merely a craft; it was a form of power. The ability to forge weapons, tools, and sacred objects gave the Kenites influence disproportionate to their numbers. Likewise, scribal knowledge (the ability to record, preserve, and transmit) made them custodians of memory. In both cases, they held the keys to civilization.

The Ambiguous Role of the Kenites

The Kenites appear in Scripture as both allies and potential threats:
- Allies of Israel: Jethro, the Kenite priest of Midian, advises Moses in Exodus 18, offering wisdom that shapes Israel's governance. The Kenites travel with Judah in Judges 1:16, sharing in the conquest of Canaan.
- Ambiguous Outsiders: Balaam's oracle in Numbers 24:21–22 warns that though the Kenites dwell securely, they will eventually be consumed by Asshur. Their security is temporary, their role provisional.
- Survivors of Judgment: In 1 Samuel 15:6, Saul spares the Kenites during the destruction of Amalek, citing their kindness to Israel. Once again, they survive where others perish.

This pattern suggests that the Kenites were tolerated, even respected, but never fully integrated. They were necessary, but not entirely trusted. Their knowledge was valuable, but potentially dangerous.

The Kenites and Forbidden Knowledge

The Kenites embody the paradox of knowledge: it can preserve covenant or corrupt it. As smiths, they forged the tools of survival and the weapons of war. As scribes, they preserved sacred texts and transmitted esoteric traditions. Their lineage is a thread of continuity between the pre-Flood world of Cain and the post-Flood world of Israel.

Some traditions suggest that the Kenites preserved fragments of Watcher knowledge (metallurgy, enchantments, and hidden wisdom) passing it down through secret lineages. Others see them as faithful allies, preserving the memory of covenant alongside Israel. Both may be true. The Kenites are liminal figures, standing at the threshold between remembrance and estrangement.

The Kenite Legacy

The Kenites remind us that knowledge is never neutral. It can be used to build or to destroy, to preserve or to corrupt. Their survival across ages, their ambiguous role in Israel's story, and their association with Cain suggest that the serpent's legacy did not end with the Flood. It adapted, survived, and re-emerged through lineages like the Kenites.

The Kenite bloodline is a reminder that the battle between covenant and estrangement is not only cosmic but genealogical, not only spiritual but cultural. It is carried in bloodlines, in crafts, in texts, and in traditions. And it continues to shape history.

Chapter 4 –
Azazel and the Two Hundred

"They swore together and bound themselves by oath."
— Book of Enoch (Ethiopic tradition)

On Mount Hermon, two hundred fallen angels (Watchers) swore an oath to descend. Each taught forbidden knowledge: Azazel metallurgy, Semjaza enchantments, Penemue writing. Their offspring, the Nephilim, devoured the earth. When their bodies perished in the Flood, their spirits remained... the demons of later ages. The Watchers' rebellion was not annihilated but restrained, awaiting judgment.

The Two Hundred

The serpent's whisper in Eden was subtle. Cain's rebellion was archetypal. The Kenites preserved forbidden knowledge in the margins of history. But in the days before the Flood, estrangement escalated into open invasion. The veil between heaven and earth was pierced, and two hundred celestial beings descended upon Mount Hermon. Their leader was Semjaza, but their most infamous figure was Azazel... the one who taught men to forge weapons, adorn women, and corrupt flesh.

The fallen angels' (Watchers') descent was not myth in the sense of fiction. It was myth in the sense of memory... a record of an event so disruptive that it reshaped the trajectory of humanity. The Watchers did not merely observe; they intervened. They did not merely tempt; they instructed. And in doing so, they introduced a counterfeit civilization.

The Oath on Mount Hermon

The Book of Enoch describes the moment with precision. Two hundred angels, desiring the daughters of men, feared to act alone. Semjaza, their leader, proposed a pact: they would all swear together, binding themselves by mutual imprecations. On Mount Hermon, they sealed their oath, giving the mountain its name... "the place of the curse."

This oath was more than rebellion. It was a covenant of corruption, a mirror image of GOD's covenant with humanity. Where GOD's covenant promised life, theirs promised estrangement. Where God's covenant preserved memory, theirs sought to erase it. The Watchers became the first fraternity of rebellion, united not by obedience but by transgression.

The Forbidden Teachings

Each Watcher brought a gift — knowledge forbidden to humanity at that stage of history. These were not neutral skills; they were accelerants of corruption.

- Azazel: taught men to make swords, knives, shields, and breastplates; taught women to use cosmetics, jewelry, and enchantments. He weaponized both war and seduction.
- Semjaza: taught enchantments, root-cuttings, and sorcery.
- Baraqijal: taught astrology.
- Kokabel: taught the constellations.
- Ezeqeel: taught the knowledge of the clouds.
- Araqiel: taught the signs of the earth.
- Shamsiel: taught the signs of the sun.
- Sariel: taught the course of the moon.

These teachings were not gifts of wisdom but distortions of order.

They accelerated violence, vanity, and manipulation. They severed humanity from dependence on GOD and replaced it with dependence on systems of control.

The Birth of the Nephilim

The union of the Watchers with human women produced the Nephilim... giants, hybrids, and tyrants. They were described as "mighty men of old, men of renown." But their renown was terror. They consumed the earth's resources, enslaved populations, and turned creation into chaos. Their very existence was a corruption of flesh, a violation of the created order.

The Nephilim were not merely large in stature. They were large in appetite. 1 Enoch records that they devoured everything that men produced, then turned to devouring men themselves. They were predators, both physical and spiritual, embodying the serpent's legacy of estrangement.

Azazel's Infamy

Among the Watchers, Azazel stands apart. His teachings of warfare and seduction corrupted both men and women. He is singled out in 1 Enoch 10:8: "The whole earth has been corrupted through the works that were taught by Azazel: to him ascribe all sin." His name endures in the Day of Atonement ritual (Leviticus 16), where one goat is sacrificed to the Lord and the other (the scapegoat) is sent into the wilderness "for Azazel." This ritual preserves the memory of his corruption and the need for its removal.

Azazel represents the weaponization of knowledge. He embodies the serpent's tactic of offering power apart from purpose, beauty apart from covenant, and strength apart from obedience. His legacy is visible in every age where war and vanity dominate.

The Judgment of the Watchers

The corruption could not continue unchecked. According to 1 Enoch, GOD sent the archangels to intervene:
- Michael: bound Semjaza and the other leaders.
- Raphael: bound Azazel hand and foot, casting him into the desert and covering him with jagged rocks until the day of judgment.

- Gabriel: sent to destroy the Nephilim, setting them against one another in war.
- Uriel: warned Noah of the coming Flood.

The Watchers were supposedly bound in Tartarus, a place of chains and darkness, as echoed in 2 Peter 2:4 and Jude 1:6. Their offspring perished in the Flood, but their spirits remained... becoming the demons that plague humanity to this day.

The Legacy of the Two Hundred

The descent of the Watchers established a pattern that echoes through history:
- Knowledge as Control: Forbidden teachings become systems of domination.
- Hybridization as Corruption: The mingling of categories produces chaos.
- Judgment as Reset: When corruption reaches saturation, erasure follows.

The Watchers' legacy is visible in every empire that weaponizes knowledge, every culture that glorifies vanity, and every system that severs humanity from covenant.

Their oath on Mount Hermon was the first fraternity of rebellion, but its echoes continue in secret societies, hidden councils, and subterranean traditions.

Chapter 5 –
The Craters of Their Fall

"A star fell from heaven, blazing like a torch."
— Sibylline Oracles, Book V

Legends of fire from heaven echo across cultures. Two-hundred craters... Exactly the number of fallen angels (Watchers) who came to Earth. Myths of fiery descent align with these scars. Perhaps these are not meteor strikes but the very places where the Watchers fell, their descent etched into the earth itself.

200 Craters Worldwide

The earth is scarred with reminders of intrusion. Across continents and oceans, geologists have catalogued 190 confirmed impact craters… vast depressions formed by sudden violence from above. Yet this number is not final. At least ten more likely remain hidden beneath jungles, deserts, or the ocean floor. When ten more are discovered, the total would reach 200 , a number that resonates with the two hundred angels who descended upon Mount Hermon in the days before the Flood.

The symmetry is striking. Two hundred angels bound by oath; two hundred scars upon the earth. The vast majority of these craters are perfectly round, as though stamped into the crust by a force beyond comprehension. Roundness is the signature of descent, the mark of something falling from heaven with unimaginable velocity.

Could it be that the Watchers' fall was not only spiritual but physical? That their descent left scars upon the earth itself? The craters of their fall may be more than geological curiosities. They may be memorials of intrusion, etched into the land as testimony of rebellion.

The Roundness of Judgment

Impact craters are almost always circular, regardless of the angle of descent. This is because the energy released upon impact radiates outward in all directions, producing a symmetrical scar.

The roundness itself is symbolic: a circle is a sign of eternity, of completeness, of covenant. Yet here, the circle is inverted… a covenant of rebellion, a completeness of corruption.

The Watchers' descent was not a gentle arrival. It was a violent intrusion, a shattering of boundaries. Their fall may have been accompanied by fire, shockwaves, and the carving of round memorials into the earth. Each crater is a reminder that rebellion leaves scars, and that those scars endure.

Witnesses in Stone

Among the 190 known craters, several stand as monumental witnesses:

1. Meteor Crater (Barringer Crater), Arizona, USA — 1.2 km wide, one of the best-preserved impact craters on earth.
2. Chicxulub Crater, Yucatán Peninsula, Mexico — 180 km wide, linked to the extinction of the dinosaurs.
3. Vredefort Crater, South Africa — 300 km wide, the largest confirmed impact structure on earth.
4. Sudbury Basin, Ontario, Canada — 250 km wide, rich in nickel and copper deposits.
5. Lonar Crater, Maharashtra, India — 1.8 km wide, formed in basalt, associated with local myths of divine wrath.
6. Manicouagan Crater, Quebec, Canada — 100 km wide, now a ring-shaped lake visible from space.
7. Popigai Crater, Siberia, Russia — 100 km wide, associated with diamond deposits.
8. Kara Crater, Nenetsia, Russia — 65 km wide, partially eroded but still visible.
9. Clearwater Lakes, Quebec, Canada — twin craters, 32 km and 22 km wide, strikingly circular.

10. Wolfe Creek Crater, Western Australia — 875 m wide, preserved in desert sands, sacred in Aboriginal tradition.

Each of these sites is a scar of intrusion, a round memorial of descent. They are scattered across continents, yet united in form.

They testify that the heavens have struck the earth before... and may do so again.

The Descent of the Angels

1 Enoch describes two hundred angels descending upon Mount Hermon, bound by oath to take human wives and corrupt creation. Their descent was not metaphorical alone. It may have been accompanied by physical force... a shattering of the atmosphere, a burning of the sky, a carving of craters into the land.

Imagine two hundred beings of immense power, breaking through the veil between heaven and earth. Their arrival would not be silent. It would be cataclysmic.

Shockwaves would flatten forests. Fire would rain from the sky. The ground itself would bear the scars of their fall. The craters we see today may be the remnants of that descent, the physical testimony of a spiritual rebellion.

The Pattern of Cataclysm

The craters are not evenly distributed. Many of them cluster in regions associated with ancient civilizations, mythic traditions, and resets. Chicxulub in Mexico, near the cradle of

Mesoamerican myth. Lonar in India, tied to Hindu legends of divine wrath. Wolfe Creek in Australia, sacred to Aboriginal Dreamtime stories.

These alignments suggest that ancient peoples remembered the craters not as accidents but as acts of judgment. They wove them into their myths, their rituals, their cosmologies. The craters became sacred sites, places where heaven touched earth in fire and stone.

The Craters as Memorials of Rebellion

If the Watchers' descent was accompanied by such force, then the craters are not merely geological. They are memorials. Each round scar is a reminder of the oath on Mount Hermon, the corruption of flesh, and the judgment that followed.

The number (190 known, with perhaps 10 more hidden) mirrors the two hundred angels. The roundness mirrors the completeness of their rebellion. The global distribution mirrors the global reach of their corruption.

The craters of their fall are not silent. They speak. They testify that rebellion leaves scars, that judgment is real, and that the earth itself remembers.

Chapter 6 –
The Council Beneath the Earth

"The Ant People brought us down into the earth and saved us."
— *Hopi oral tradition*

Subterranean halls appear in global traditions: Cappadocia's underground cities, Hopi "Ant People," hollow hills of Europe. These echo the Watchers' retreat underground after the Flood. Their council chamber, remembered as the Table of Two Hundred, was a device of resonance, issuing edicts through Kenite stewards above and reptiloid (humanoid reptilian) custodians below. A hidden triad of control was born.

Hidden Councils

The Watchers' descent was not only a rebellion in the heavens; it was the beginning of hidden councils on earth. When their offspring perished in the Flood, and when the angels themselves were bound in chains, their influence did not vanish. Instead, it retreated. It went underground, literally and figuratively.

From the earliest myths to modern folklore, humanity has preserved memory of subterranean beings, hidden cities, and councils that govern in secrecy. These traditions suggest that beneath the surface of the earth lies a shadow world ... a place where remnants of ancient knowledge, forbidden archives, and estranged powers continue their work away from the eyes of men.

The Biblical Hints of Hidden Councils

Scripture itself hints at hidden assemblies. Psalm 82 describes GOD standing in the "divine council" and judging among the gods. Isaiah 29:15 warns: "Woe unto them that seek deep to hide their counsel from the LORD, and their works are in the dark." Ezekiel 8 describes secret chambers beneath the Temple where elders worship idols in darkness.

These passages suggest that rebellion is not only cosmic but subterranean... hidden councils plotting beneath the surface, away from the light of covenant. The imagery of "depths" and "darkness" recurs throughout the Bible as a metaphor for secrecy, corruption, and estrangement.

Subterranean Cities in Myth and Tradition

Across cultures, myths of underground cities and councils abound:
- Hopi Tradition (North America): The Ant People sheltered humanity underground during previous cataclysms, teaching survival and preserving memory.
- Greek Myth: Hades rules the underworld, a subterranean realm where councils of the dead and chthonic gods convene.
- Norse Myth: Svartálfaheimr, the realm of the dwarves, is a subterranean world of smiths and hidden knowledge.
- Hindu Tradition: The Nagas dwell in Pātāla, a vast underground kingdom filled with treasures and guarded secrets.
- Tibetan & Central Asian Lore: Shambhala and Agartha are said to be hidden subterranean realms where councils of enlightened or estranged beings rule in secrecy.

These traditions converge on a single theme: beneath the earth lies a hidden order, a council of beings who preserve knowledge, wealth, and power away from the surface world.

Archaeological Anomalies

The earth itself bears witness to subterranean mysteries:
- Derinkuyu, Cappadocia (Turkey): A vast underground city capable of housing tens of thousands, complete with ventilation shafts, wells, and defensive mechanisms.

- Hypogeum of Hal-Saflieni (Malta): A subterranean temple complex with acoustic properties, associated with ritual and burial.
- Chavín de Huántar (Peru): Underground galleries and labyrinths used for ritual initiation.
- Ellora and Ajanta Caves (India): Rock-cut temples and monasteries, suggesting ancient subterranean engineering.
- Naours Tunnels (France): A subterranean city used across centuries, rediscovered in modern times.

These sites demonstrate that subterranean habitation and councils are not merely myth. They are historical realities, though their purposes (survival, ritual, secrecy) can vary.

The Council as Custodians of Memory

If the Watchers' knowledge survived the Flood, it may have been preserved in subterranean councils. The Kenites, as smiths and scribes, may have been intermediaries. The Nephilim spirits, restless and bodiless, may have haunted underground chambers. The councils beneath the earth may have served as custodians of forbidden archives... metallurgy, enchantments, astronomy, and genetic manipulation.

These councils are not necessarily unified. Some traditions describe them as benevolent (the Ant People, Shambhala), while others portray them as malevolent (Hades, Tartarus, Agartha's darker legends). What unites them is secrecy, depth, and the preservation of knowledge away from the surface world.

The Modern Echoes

Even in modern times, the myth of subterranean councils persists. Conspiracy traditions speak of underground bases, hidden archives, and councils of elites who govern from the shadows. While often dismissed, these echoes resonate with ancient memory: the idea that beneath the surface lies a hidden order, a council of estrangement, a continuation of the Watchers' rebellion.

The serpent's legacy is not only in the heavens or on the surface. It is beneath our feet, in chambers of stone, in archives of secrecy, in councils that plot in darkness.

The Council Beneath the Earth as Archetype

The archetype of the subterranean council represents estrangement hidden from sight. It is the inversion of the divine council, which operates in light and truth. The subterranean council operates in darkness and secrecy. It is the shadow of covenant, the counterfeit of remembrance.

To expose it is to remember. To remember is to resist. The councils beneath the earth may remain hidden, but their influence is felt in every age where secrecy governs, where archives are suppressed, and where power is wielded in darkness.

Chapter 7 –
The Council Beneath the Earth (Expanded)

"The hollow hills are filled with kings who sleep until the end of days."
— Celtic folklore

The Watchers' survival after the Flood ensured their influence endured. Not all were bound; some remained hidden. Their subterranean halls became centers of command. The Table of Two Hundred was their nexus, a metallic construct echoing the Ark's dangerous power and Delphi's oracles. Through it, they coordinated their hidden governance.

Hidden Counterfeit Assembly

The previous chapter traced the memory of subterranean realms... hidden cities, labyrinths, and chambers beneath the earth. But the question remains: who inhabits these depths, and what councils convene there?

The biblical witness, apocryphal traditions, and comparative mythology converge on a startling theme: beneath the surface of the earth, councils of estranged powers gather. They are not merely mythic beings of folklore, but archetypes of rebellion, secrecy, and control. These councils are the shadow of the DIVINE council... a counterfeit assembly that operates in darkness rather than light.

The Archetype of the Hidden Council

The DIVINE council, as described in Psalm 82 and Job 1, is a heavenly assembly where GOD presides among HIS host. The subterranean council is its inversion. Where the DIVINE council governs in light, the hidden council governs in secrecy. Where the DIVINE council preserves covenant, the hidden council plots estrangement.

This archetype recurs across cultures: a secret assembly beneath the earth, ruling unseen, preserving forbidden knowledge, and influencing the surface world through intermediaries.

Biblical and Apocryphal Allusions

- Ezekiel 8: Elders of Israel worship idols in hidden chambers beneath the Temple.

- Isaiah 29:15: Woe to those who "seek deep to hide their counsel from the Lord."
- 1 Enoch 10–15: The Watchers are bound in subterranean prisons, yet their spirits continue to influence humanity.
- Jubilees 5: The angels who sinned are confined in the depths until judgment.
- Revelation 9: The abyss is opened, releasing locust-like beings under the command of Abaddon.

These texts suggest that beneath the earth lies not only imprisonment but counsel, assemblies of estranged powers who continue to plot against covenant.

The Composition of the Subterranean Council

Traditions describe the subterranean council as a composite of beings:
- Bound Watchers: Imprisoned in Tartarus, yet still exerting influence through intermediaries.
- Nephilim Spirits: Restless, bodiless, seeking embodiment, whispering in darkness.
- Human Intermediaries: Lineages such as the Kenites, scribes and smiths who preserve forbidden knowledge.
- Reptiloid humanoid species from the first Earth Age (one was the father of Kenites... Cain).
- Chthonic Deities: In Greek myth, Hades and Persephone; in Hindu lore, the Nagas; in Norse myth, Hel and her court.
- Hidden Kings: Folklore of sleeping kings beneath mountains (Arthur, Barbarossa, Charlemagne) suggests councils of rulers awaiting return.

Together, these figures form a shadow assembly... a council of estrangement that mirrors the DIVINE council above.

Agendas of the Hidden Council

The subterranean council is not passive. Its agendas, drawn from myth and scripture, include:
1. Preservation of Forbidden Knowledge: Metallurgy, enchantments, astronomy, genetic manipulation.
2. Manipulation of Surface Civilizations: Whispering into kings, priests, and scribes; influencing law, war, and ritual.
3. Guardianship of Hidden Archives: Subterranean libraries, sealed chambers, and lost technologies.
4. Preparation for Return: Legends of sleeping kings and imprisoned beings suggest a future re-emergence.
5. Counterfeit Covenant: Establishing systems of control that mimic divine order but enslave rather than liberate.

Subterranean Councils in World Myth

These myths are not identical, but they have similarities. They preserve memory of councils beneath the earth, operating in secrecy, influencing the surface world.

- Hopi Ant People: Councils beneath the earth who preserved humanity during cataclysm.
- Greek Hades: A court of judges and rulers beneath the earth.
- Norse Hel: A subterranean realm where councils of the dead convene.

- Hindu Pātāla: Ruled by serpent-kings (Nagas), filled with treasures and secret knowledge.
- Tibetan Shambhala / Agartha: Hidden councils of rulers beneath the Himalayas, guiding or deceiving humanity.

Archaeological Echoes

These sites demonstrate that subterranean councils are not only mythic but historical. Humanity has repeatedly built chambers beneath the earth for ritual, secrecy, and governance.

- Derinkuyu (Turkey): Multi-level underground city, capable of housing tens of thousands.
- Hypogeum of Hal-Saflieni (Malta): Subterranean temple with acoustic resonance, suggesting ritual councils.
- Chavín de Huántar (Peru): Underground galleries used for initiation and altered states.
- Ellora and Ajanta (India): Rock-cut subterranean temples, centers of hidden ritual.
- Naours Tunnels (France): Subterranean city rediscovered, used across centuries.

Modern Echoes of the Subterranean Council

In modern times, the archetype persists in conspiracy traditions: underground bases, hidden archives, councils of elites who govern from the shadows. While often dismissed, these echoes resonate with ancient memory. They suggest that the archetype of the subterranean council is alive, a pattern that recurs whenever secrecy and estrangement dominate.

The serpent's legacy is not only in Eden, not only in the heavens, but beneath our feet. The councils beneath the earth are the shadow of covenant, the counterfeit of remembrance, the hidden assemblies of estrangement.

The Council Beneath the Earth as Warning

The subterranean council is not merely myth. It is a warning. It reminds us that rebellion hides, that estrangement plots in darkness, that forbidden knowledge is preserved in secret. It reminds us that the battle is not only visible but hidden, not only on the surface but beneath it.

To remember is to resist. To expose the councils beneath the earth is to break their secrecy. To walk in covenant is to reject their counterfeit. The councils may remain hidden, but their influence is not. And their judgment is certain.

Chapter 8 –
Kenites as Stewards of Civilization

"The scribe is the memory of kings."
— Ancient Egyptian maxim

The Kenites, smiths and scribes, became the visible face of the Watchers' hidden hand. By controlling tools and texts, they shaped civilizations without armies. They reappear in every age: metallurgists, financiers, bureaucrats, technocrats. Always indispensable, never fully integrated, always adjacent to covenant but estranged from it.

Shaping Civilization

The Kenites are one of the most enigmatic lineages in the biblical record. Descended, by name and tradition, from Cain (Qayin), they appear at key junctures in Israel's story... never central, yet never absent. They are wanderers, smiths, scribes, and priests. They are both kin and stranger, both ally and outsider.

The Kenites embody the paradox of knowledge: they are stewards of civilization, preserving crafts and texts essential to human flourishing, yet their lineage is shadowed by Cain, the archetype of rebellion. To understand the Kenites is to understand how forbidden knowledge survived the Flood, how it was transmitted into Israel's orbit, and how it shaped the civilizations of the ancient Near East.

The Kenites in the Biblical Record

The Kenites appear in several key passages:
- Genesis 4:22 — Tubal-Cain, a descendant of Cain, is described as "an instructor of every artificer in brass and iron." This establishes the Cainite tradition of metallurgy.
- Genesis 15:19 — The Kenites are listed among the peoples inhabiting the land promised to Abraham.
- Exodus 18 — Jethro, Moses' father-in-law, is a priest of Midian and identified with the Kenites. He advises Moses on governance, shaping Israel's judicial system.
- Judges 1:16 — The Kenites travel with Judah into Canaan, dwelling among the people.
- 1 Samuel 15:6 — Saul spares the Kenites during the destruction of Amalek, citing their kindness to Israel.

- Numbers 24:21–22 — Balaam prophesies concerning the Kenites: "Strong is thy dwelling place, and thou puttest thy nest in a rock. Nevertheless the Kenite shall be wasted, until Asshur shall carry thee away captive."

These passages portray the Kenites as liminal figures… present, influential, yet never fully integrated into Israel.

The Kenites as Metallurgists

The Kenites inherited the craft of Tubal-Cain, the first smith. Metallurgy was not merely a practical skill; it was sacred knowledge. To forge metal was to harness fire, to transform earth into weapon or tool, to mediate between raw creation and human civilization.

In ancient cultures, smiths were often liminal figures… feared, revered, and sometimes marginalized. They were seen as wielders of dangerous knowledge, intermediaries between the human and the divine. The Kenites, as smiths, carried this aura. They were indispensable to kings and armies, yet always outsiders.

The Kenites as Scribes

Beyond metallurgy, the Kenites are associated with writing and record-keeping. In the ancient Near East, scribes were custodians of memory, shaping the narratives of kings and gods. The Kenites, as scribes, may have preserved fragments of pre-Flood knowledge, transmitting them into Israel's orbit.

Karel van der Toorn notes that scribal culture was not neutral; it was formative. To write was to shape reality, to fix memory, to control narrative. The Kenites, as scribes, were not merely recorders but some of the shapers of civilization.

The Kenites as Priests and Advisors

Jethro, the Kenite priest of Midian, plays a pivotal role in Israel's story. In Exodus 18, he advises Moses to establish a system of judges, delegating authority and preventing burnout. This counsel shapes Israel's governance, embedding Kenite wisdom into covenantal structure.

The Kenites thus appear not only as craftsmen and scribes but as priests and advisors... mediators of wisdom, shaping Israel from the margins.

The Ambiguity of the Kenites

The Kenites embody ambiguity:
- Allies of Israel: They travel with Judah, advise Moses, and are spared by Saul.
- Outsiders: They are never fully integrated, always distinct, always liminal.
- Stewards of Knowledge: They preserve metallurgy, writing, and governance.
- Shadowed by Cain: Their lineage recalls the first murderer, the archetype of rebellion.

This ambiguity reflects the paradox of knowledge itself: it can preserve covenant or corrupt it, build civilization or enslave it.

The Kenites and Civilization

The Kenites functioned as stewards of civilization. Their crafts, texts, and counsel shaped the ancient Near East. They were intermediaries between hidden councils and surface kings, between forbidden knowledge and covenantal law.

Civilization requires memory, craft, and governance. The Kenites provided all three. Yet their role was never neutral. They were stewards of knowledge, but knowledge itself is double-edged. It can illuminate or obscure, liberate or enslave.

The Legacy of the Kenites

The Kenites remind us that civilization is built not only by kings and armies but by craftsmen, scribes, and advisors. They are the hidden stewards, the marginal figures whose knowledge shapes nations.

Their legacy is ambiguous, but it is enduring. They are the shadow lineage of Cain, yet they are also allies of Israel. They are outsiders, yet they shape the inside. They are stewards of civilization, yet their stewardship is always tinged with estrangement.

Chapter 9 –
Fires and Floods of Memory

"The city was consumed by fire, and its people scattered like ashes."
— *Babylonian Chronicle*

Resets recur through history: the Great Fire of London (1666), the Chicago Fire (1871), the San Francisco Earthquake and Fire (1906). Each erased archives, destroyed property records, and enabled new systems. Alternative researchers point to the "mud flood" hypothesis (buried cities, orphan trains, world's fairs) as evidence of deliberate erasure. Whether mainstream or fringe, the pattern is clear: memory erased, systems rebuilt.

Catastrophes Throughout History

Humanity's memory is shaped by catastrophe. Floods and fires are not only natural disasters; they are instruments of divine judgment, cosmic resets, and cultural erasures. They destroy archives, scatter populations, and force civilizations to begin anew. Yet paradoxically, they also preserve memory through myth, ritual, and scarred landscapes.

The Bible, apocryphal texts, and world mythologies all testify to this dual role of cataclysm: to erase and to remember. The Flood of Noah erased a corrupted world, yet preserved covenantal lineage. The fire that consumed Sodom erased a city, yet it left a testimony of judgment. Ancient myths of deluge and conflagration echo across continents, suggesting that humanity remembers through the very events that destroy.

The Flood as Erasure and Preservation

The Flood of Genesis 6–9 is the archetype of watery judgment. It erased a world corrupted by the Watchers and the Nephilim, yet preserved Noah, his family, and the blueprint of creation. The ark functioned as a vessel of memory, carrying forward the covenantal line, clean animals, and the possibility of renewal.

Other cultures preserve parallel flood traditions:
- Mesopotamia: The Epic of Gilgamesh describes Utnapishtim surviving a great flood in a vessel, preserving life.
- Sumerian King List: Records kingship before and after a great flood.
- Hopi Tradition: Humanity is saved from flood by retreating underground with the Ant People.

- Mesoamerican Myths: Speak of previous worlds destroyed by water.

The flood is remembered not only as destruction but as preservation — a paradoxical act of erasure that ensures continuity.

Fire as Judgment and Memory

If water erases, fire purifies. The Bible repeatedly portrays fire as an instrument of judgment:

- Genesis 19: Sodom and Gomorrah consumed by fire from heaven.
- Exodus 19: Mount Sinai enveloped in fire as GOD descends.
- 2 Kings 1: Fire from heaven consumes captains and their men.
- 2 Peter 3: The present world is reserved for fire, just as the former world was destroyed by water.

Fire destroys archives, cities, and civilizations. Yet it also leaves enduring memory. The ruins of Pompeii, preserved in volcanic ash, testify to sudden destruction. The Great Fire of London (1666) erased medieval London but gave birth to a new city. The Great Fire of Chicago (1871) destroyed thousands of buildings but became a mythic symbol of rebirth.

Fire is both erasure and remembrance. It destroys, but it also sears memory into stone, ash, and story.

The Cycle of Flood and Fire

There seems to be an established cosmic cycle: the world that was perished by water; the world that is will perish by fire. This cycle is echoed in myth:

- Hindu Cosmology: The world ends alternately in fire and flood, in cycles of destruction and renewal.
- Norse Myth: Ragnarök ends with fire consuming the world, followed by renewal.
- Zoroastrian Tradition: The world will be purified by molten metal, a fiery flood.

Flood and fire are not random. They are cyclical and remembered across cultures as the mechanisms by which history is reset.

Fires and Floods as Cultural Resets

Throughout history, fires and floods have functioned as cultural resets:

- The Library of Alexandria: Destroyed by fire, erasing vast archives of ancient knowledge.
- The Flood of the Nile: Annual inundations both destroyed and renewed Egyptian civilization.
- The Yellow River Floods (China): Catastrophic floods reshaped dynasties and myth.
- The San Francisco Earthquake and Fire (1906): Destroyed archives, reshaped the city, and erased inconvenient records.

Each event erased memory, yet also created new narratives. Fires and floods are not only disasters; they are instruments of historical editing.

The Memory of Cataclysm

Humanity remembers cataclysm through myth, ritual, and scarred landscapes:
- Myth: Flood and fire stories across cultures preserve memory of resets.
- Ritual: Festivals of fire (e.g., Beltane, Diwali) and water (e.g., baptism, purification rites) reenact cosmic cycles.
- Landscapes: Craters, floodplains, and ruins serve as physical memorials.

Memory is paradoxical: it survives through erasure. Fires and floods destroy, yet they also ensure that humanity never forgets.

Fires and Floods of the Future

If the past was erased by water, and the present is reserved for fire, then the future holds another reset. The councils beneath the earth may preserve forbidden knowledge, but fire will test it. Archives may be hidden, but fire will expose them. The serpent's legacy may endure, but fire will consume it.

The fires and floods of memory remind us that history is not linear but cyclical, not secure but fragile. They remind us that covenant endures, even when civilizations perish. They remind us that remembrance is forged in the crucible of erasure.

Chapter 10 –
World Wars as Rituals of Pruning

"War is the father of all things."
— *Heraclitus*

World War I dissolved empires; World War II obliterated cities. Dresden, Tokyo, Hiroshima... firestorms and even nuclear light all worked to erased millions. Out of the ashes arose the League of Nations, the United Nations, the IMF (International Monetary Fund), the World Bank. Wars functioned as rituals of pruning: populations culled, archives destroyed, systems reset. The Watchers' ancient method perfected in geopolitics.

The Twentieth Century

The twentieth century was defined by two global conflagrations: the First and Second World Wars. Together, they reshaped borders, toppled empires, erased archives, and reordered civilization. Yet beyond their political and military dimensions, these wars can be read as rituals of pruning... cataclysmic events that cut away populations, traditions, and memories, leaving behind a reshaped world.

Just as the Flood erased a corrupted world and fire consumed Sodom, the World Wars functioned as modern resets. They pruned humanity, not only through death but through the destruction of archives, the displacement of peoples, and the imposition of new systems. They were not accidents of history but key world events, echoing the cycles of erasure and remembrance that have defined human civilization since antiquity.

The First World War: The End of Empires

The First World War (1914–1918) was a pruning of empires. The Austro-Hungarian, Ottoman, German, and Russian empires collapsed. Monarchies that had ruled for centuries were swept away. The war consumed nearly 20 million lives and displaced millions more.

But beyond the human toll, the war erased archives, traditions, and ways of life. Entire villages in France and Belgium were obliterated. Libraries, churches, and cultural centers were destroyed. The war introduced mechanized slaughter... machine guns, poison gas, tanks... technologies that transformed killing into an industry.

The pruning was not only physical but cultural. The old order of Europe was cut down, making way for new ideologies: communism, fascism, nationalism. The war was a scythe, cutting away the old to prepare the ground for the new.

The Second World War: The Fire of Total War

If the First World War pruned empires, the Second World War (1939–1945) pruned civilizations. With over 70 million dead, it was the deadliest conflict in human history. Cities were reduced to ash: Warsaw, Dresden, Hiroshima, Nagasaki. Archives were burned, art looted, populations displaced.

The Holocaust was a pruning of people and memory… an attempt to erase entire lineages, traditions, and histories. The atomic bomb was a fiery reset, introducing humanity to apocalyptic power. The war ended with the world divided into two superpowers, the United States and the Soviet Union, inaugurating a new order.

The pruning was total. It cut not only populations but the very imagination of humanity. After Hiroshima, the possibility of global annihilation became part of human consciousness. The war was both fire and flood… consuming, erasing, and reshaping.

War as Ritual

Why describe these wars as rituals of pruning? Because they follow the seemingly endless pattern of cataclysm:
- Sacrifice: Millions of lives offered on the altar of ideology and empire.
- Erasure: Archives, cities, and traditions destroyed.

- Purification: Old orders swept away, new systems imposed.
- Memory: Monuments, myths, and rituals of remembrance created.

War functions as ritual when it is not only fought but commemorated, when its destruction is framed as necessary for renewal, when its victims are memorialized as sacrifices for a new order. The World Wars were not only battles; they were rituals of global transformation.

The Pruning of Archives

One of the most overlooked aspects of the World Wars is the destruction of archives. Libraries in Louvain, Warsaw, and Berlin were burned. Records of entire communities were lost. The war erased not only lives but memories, severing lineages and traditions.

This pruning of archives echoes the burning of the Library of Alexandria, the destruction of Jerusalem's Temple, and the erasures of fire and flood in antiquity. War is not only about territory; it is about memory. To prune archives is to prune identity.

The Pruning of Populations

The wars pruned populations in multiple ways:
- Death: Tens of millions killed in battle, bombing, genocide.
- Displacement: Refugees scattered across continents.
- Assimilation: Survivors absorbed into new nations, losing languages and traditions.

- Selection: Certain lineages targeted for erasure, others preserved for power.

This pruning was not random. It was selective, shaping the genetic, cultural, and political landscape of the modern world.

The Pruning of Civilizations

The wars pruned civilizations themselves. The Ottoman Empire, with its centuries of Islamic rule, was cut down. The Austro-Hungarian Empire, with its patchwork of peoples, was erased. The British Empire, though victorious, was pruned of its global dominance.

Civilizations are pruned when their institutions collapse, their traditions are forgotten, and their people are scattered. The World Wars were not only battles of armies but scythes cutting through civilizations.

The Legacy of the Pruning

The legacy of the World Wars is paradoxical. They destroyed, yet they also created. They erased, yet they also preserved. They pruned, yet they also prepared the ground for new growth.

The United Nations, the European Union, the Cold War order... all emerged from the pruning. The wars remind us that cataclysm is both end and beginning, both erasure and remembrance. They are modern echoes of the Flood and the fire, rituals of pruning that shaped the world we inhabit.

Chapter 11 –
The Problem of Nephilim Spirits

"The restless dead wander the earth, seeking bodies to inhabit."
— *Akkadian incantation tablet*

The Flood destroyed bodies but not spirits. The Nephilim became demons... restless, bodiless, hungry. Cultures worldwide describe them: Babylonian utukku, Greek daimones, Hebrew shedim, Arabic djinn. Possession was unstable; human vessels burned out. The Watchers required new vessels.

Nephilim Spirits With Nowhere to Go

The Flood erased the corrupted flesh of the Nephilim... the hybrid offspring of the Watchers and human women. But it did not erase their spirits. According to ancient texts, when the bodies of the giants perished, their spirits remained. These disembodied entities, born of rebellion and estrangement, became the evil spirits that plague humanity.

This chapter explores the problem of Nephilim spirits: their origin, nature, behavior, and influence. It traces how these spirits became the restless agents of corruption, whispering into kings, haunting ruins, and perpetuating the legacy of the Watchers long after their (the Nephilim's) physical destruction.

The Origin of Nephilim Spirits

The Book of Enoch provides the clearest account. In chapters 15–16, GOD addresses the Watchers directly, explaining that their offspring (the Nephilim) are not part of the divine order. When their bodies die, their spirits do not ascend. Thus their spirits had nowhere to go. Instead, they remain on earth as evil spirits, bound to wander, afflict, and corrupt.

These spirits are described as:
- Restless: Unable to find peace, perpetually seeking embodiment.
- Malevolent: Born of rebellion, they hate humanity and seek its destruction.
- Influential: They whisper into minds, stir up violence, and perpetuate estrangement.

Unlike demons in later theology, Nephilim spirits are not fallen angels. They are the disembodied remnants of hybrid beings... neither fully divine nor fully human, but corrupted echoes of both.

The Nature of Nephilim Spirits

Nephilim spirits are characterized by:
- Disembodiment: They lack physical form, yet they seek vessels — humans, animals, even objects.
- Territoriality: They haunt specific regions, ruins, or bloodlines.
- Aggression: They incite war, violence, and rebellion.
- Deception: They masquerade as gods, ancestors, or voices of enlightenment.

Their behavior mirrors the corruption of their origin. Just as the Watchers taught forbidden knowledge, Nephilim spirits perpetuate forbidden influence... not through instruction, but through possession, manipulation, and haunting.

Nephilim Spirits in Scripture

While the term "Nephilim spirits" does not appear in the canonical Bible, their presence is implied:
- Genesis 6:4 — "There were giants in the earth in those days... and also after that."
- Deuteronomy 2–3 — References to Rephaim, Anakim, and other giant clans post-Flood.
- 1 Samuel 17 — Goliath, a giant of Gath, possibly descended from Nephilim lineages.
- Mark 5:1–20 — The Gerasene demoniac, possessed by "Legion," a multitude of spirits.

- Matthew 12:43–45 — Jesus describes unclean spirits wandering through dry places, seeking rest.

These passages suggest that the spirits of the giants survived the Flood and continued to influence history... not as flesh, but as disembodied forces.

Nephilim Spirits in Apocryphal and Rabbinic Tradition

These texts portray Nephilim spirits as persistent, dangerous, and central to the spiritual warfare of humanity:
- 1 Enoch 15–16 — Evil spirits of the giants shall afflict, oppress, and destroy.
- Jubilees 10 — Noah prays for protection against the spirits of the giants; GOD binds 90% of them, leaving 10% to test humanity.
- Dead Sea Scrolls (Book of Giants) — Describes the dreams and fears of the giants before the Flood.
- Rabbinic Midrash — Some traditions suggest that Og, king of Bashan, survived the Flood by clinging to the ark, preserving Nephilim influence.

Nephilim Spirits in World Mythology

Across cultures, echoes of Nephilim spirits appear:
- Mesopotamian Pazuzu — A wind demon, restless and malevolent.
- Greek Titans and Gigantes — Defeated by the gods, yet their spirits linger in Tartarus.
- Norse Draugr — Undead warriors, haunting burial mounds.

- Hindu Asuras — Powerful spirits born of divine rebellion.
- Mesoamerican Tzitzimime — Star demons who descend during eclipses to devour humanity.

These beings share traits with Nephilim spirits: disembodiment, aggression, and influence. They are remembered not as gods, but as corrupted forces.

The Influence of Nephilim Spirits

Nephilim spirits influence history through:
- Possession: Entering individuals to incite violence, madness, or rebellion.
- Haunting: Occupying ruins, battlefields, or cursed objects.
- Whispering: Inspiring ideologies, rituals, or technologies that sever humanity from covenant.
- Bloodlines: Attaching to families or lineages that preserve forbidden knowledge.

Their influence is subtle but persistent. They do not build empires, but they whisper into those who do. They do not write laws, but they inspire those who twist them.

The Problem of Containment

Ancient texts describe attempts to contain Nephilim spirits:
- Binding: GOD binds 90% of them in Jubilees; the remaining 10% test humanity.
- Exorcism: Jesus and the apostles cast out spirits, restoring peace.

- Ritual: Cultures develop purification rites, burial practices, and taboos to ward off spirits.
- Architecture: Temples, tombs, and sacred spaces are designed to trap or repel spirits.

Yet containment is never permanent. Nephilim spirits adapt, migrate, and reemerge. They are the persistent problem of estrangement... the legacy of rebellion that refuses to die.

Nephilim Spirits and Modernity

In modern times, Nephilim spirits are reinterpreted:
- Psychology: As archetypes of trauma, rage, or madness.
- Paranormal Studies: As poltergeists, shadow beings, or residual hauntings.
- Conspiracy Traditions: As hidden influencers behind secret societies or elite bloodlines.
- Spiritual Warfare: As forces that must be discerned, resisted, and cast out.

Their names may change, but their influence remains. They are the restless echoes of a forgotten war... the disembodied agents of estrangement.

The Problem of Nephilim Spirits

The problem is not merely theological or mythic. It is existential. Nephilim spirits represent the enduring legacy of rebellion... a corruption that survives even after judgment. They are the whisper in the dark, the rage without cause, the knowledge without covenant.

To confront them is to remember. To remember is to resist. The problem of Nephilim spirits is not solved by denial, but by discernment. They are real... in the flesh (as we will soon learn), and as influence. And their judgment is not yet complete.

Chapter 12 – Engineering the Greys

"The gods mingled their seed with mortals, and giants were born."
— Hesiod, Theogony

The solution for the spirits of the Nephilim was engineered vessels: the Greys. Small, pale, large-eyed, emotionless, telepathic. Modern UFO lore (Roswell, the Hill abduction, Strieber's Communion) describes them. They are not extraterrestrials but Nephilim spirits reborn in engineered flesh. Their purpose is the same: to corrupt, to control, to sever covenant.

The Destroyed Bodies of the Nephilim

The Flood destroyed the bodies of the Nephilim, but not their spirits. These disembodied entities (born of rebellion, neither fully angelic nor fully human) were condemned to wander the earth as evil spirits. They are what later traditions call demons: restless, bodiless, and perpetually seeking embodiment.

But embodiment requires vessels. And here lies the dark genius of the Watchers' forbidden technology: the creation of engineered genetic forms... the beings we now call the Greys.

These small, humanoid entities are not extraterrestrial visitors, but synthetic bodies designed for Nephilim spirits to inhabit. They are the counterfeit flesh of estrangement, engineered to give demons form, function, and influence in the modern world.

The Greys as Engineered Vessels

Descriptions of the Greys are consistent across cultures and decades: diminutive stature, large heads, black almond-shaped eyes, grey skin, and emotionless demeanor. These traits are not evolutionary accidents... they are design features:

- Large heads: Engineered for expanded neural capacity and telepathic interfacing.
- Black eyes: Biological lenses, shielding or amplifying perception beyond the human spectrum.
- Thin bodies: Optimized for efficiency, not strength or endurance.
- Emotionless faces: Reflecting the absence of soul, empathy, or covenant.

The Greys are not alive in the human sense. They are biological drones, vessels awaiting occupation. Their purpose is not creativity or covenant, but habitation by Nephilim spirits.

Demons in Flesh

The Book of Enoch explains that the spirits of the giants became evil spirits upon the earth. These spirits are restless, destructive, and hungry for embodiment. The Greys provide that embodiment.

When Nephilim spirits inhabit these engineered forms, they gain:
- Physical Presence: The ability to interact with the material world.
- Continuity: A body that can be replaced or replicated when damaged.
- Deception: A humanoid form that mimics life but lacks soul.
- Agency: The capacity to manipulate, abduct, and experiment.

Thus, the Greys are not aliens. They are demons in engineered flesh. They are the continuation of the Nephilim problem, adapted for the modern age.

The Watchers' Technology

The Watchers, before their binding, taught forbidden arts: metallurgy, enchantments, astronomy, and genetic manipulation. Their technology was not destroyed by the Flood. It was preserved in subterranean councils, hidden archives, and bloodline traditions.

The engineering of the Greys represents the apex of this technology:

- Genetic Engineering: Creating bodies without souls, optimized for habitation.
- Hybridization: Blending human DNA with synthetic design to create vessels.
- Telepathic Networks: Linking Greys into hive-like consciousness, controlled by Nephilim spirits.
- Illusionary Projection: Crafting "alien" appearances to confound and deceive mankind.

This technology is not neutral… it is weaponized. It is designed to confound, control, and counterfeit.

Alien Deception

The Greys are central to the Watchers' plot of alien deception. By presenting themselves as extraterrestrials, they achieve several goals:

- Confusion: Distracting humanity from their true origin as Nephilim spirits.
- Displacement: Replacing biblical cosmology with narratives of "space brothers" and "galactic councils."
- Control: Using abduction, genetic sampling, and manipulation to instill fear and compliance.
- Counterfeit Revelation: Preparing humanity for a false disclosure, where "aliens" are presented as saviors rather than demons.

This deception is not accidental, it is strategic. It is designed to sever humanity from covenantal memory and replace it with counterfeit myth.

Infiltration of the Military-Industrial Complex

The Greys have not remained in folklore. They have infiltrated the structures of power. Reports from the mid-20th century onward describe:
- Crash Retrievals: Alleged recovery of Grey bodies and craft by military forces.
- Underground Bases: Facilities where Greys and humans collaborate in secrecy.
- Technology Exchange: Advanced technologies (microchips, fiber optics, stealth) allegedly reverse-engineered from Grey craft.
- Military Abductions (MILABs): Joint operations where abductees encounter both Greys and human personnel.

The military-industrial complex, whether knowingly or deceived, has become entangled in the Watchers' agenda. The Greys are not allies, they are infiltrators. Their technology is a Trojan horse, designed to ensnare humanity in systems of control.

The Deception of UFO Experts

UFO researchers, often sincere seekers of truth, have been misled by the alien deception. By framing the Greys as extraterrestrials, the true nature of the phenomenon is obscured. The result is:
- Misinterpretation: Viewing Greys as advanced beings rather than engineered vessels.
- Distraction: Focusing on "space travel" rather than spiritual warfare.
- Division: Endless debates over sightings, crashes, and disclosure, while the deeper truth is ignored.

- Preparation for False Disclosure: Conditioning humanity to accept the Greys as saviors or guides.

The serpent's legacy thrives in ambiguity. By deceiving experts, the Greys ensure that the true narrative (demons in engineered flesh) is dismissed as fringe.

The Greys as the Apex of Estrangement

The Greys represent the culmination of estrangement:
- Soulless Bodies: Flesh without covenant.
- Demonic Inhabitants: Spirits of the Nephilim, restless and destructive.
- Counterfeit Angels: Mimicking messengers of light, but serving darkness.
- Alien Deception: Replacing remembrance with confusion.
- Technological Trojan Horse: Infiltrating power structures with forbidden knowledge.

They are the serpent's legacy in modern form… engineered, deceptive, and estranged.

Resistance to the Grey Deception

To resist the Greys is to remember:
- Discernment: Recognizing that "aliens" are demons in engineered flesh.
- Covenant: Preserving divine relationship against counterfeit narratives.
- Truth: Exposing the deception of alien saviors.
- Memory: Preserving archives, traditions, and testimonies of covenant.

- Authority: Exercising spiritual authority over demons, regardless of their engineered form.

The Greys are not invincible. They are engineered. And what is engineered can be dismantled through remembrance, covenant, and truth.

Chapter 13 – Subterranean Custodians

"The earth is hollow, and within it dwell the ancients." — Norse saga fragment

The Greys are linked to underground bases: Dulce, Mount Shasta, Cappadocia. Abduction accounts describe genetic sampling, implantation, hybridization ... echoes of Genesis 6.

The goal remains unchanged: to corrupt flesh, to create a lineage estranged from GOD.

Seeking Embodiment

The Flood was meant to erase the corruption of flesh, yet the problem of estrangement did not end. The spirits of the Nephilim (the hybrid offspring of the Watchers and human women) remained on earth as demons, restless and bodiless. For millennia they have sought embodiment, vessels through which they might once again corrupt creation.

In the modern age, these vessels also appear in the form of the Greys: engineered biological forms, optimized for habitation by Nephilim spirits. Their presence is not random. They are linked to subterranean bases, hidden complexes beneath mountains, deserts, and ancient cities, where forbidden technologies are preserved and deployed. These bases function as custodial vaults, where the serpent's legacy is guarded, refined, and unleashed.

The abduction accounts of the last century (describing genetic sampling, implantation, and hybridization) are not new. They are the modern echo of Genesis 6, the continuation of the Watchers' project to corrupt flesh and create a lineage estranged from GOD.

The Greys and Underground Facilities

The Greys are consistently associated with subterranean locations. These bases are not merely military installations. They are custodial chambers, where ancient agendas are preserved.

- Dulce Base (New Mexico, USA): Alleged to be a joint human-Grey facility, deep beneath Archuleta Mesa. Reports describe genetic laboratories, vats of hybrid embryos, and experiments echoing the forbidden arts of the Watchers.

- Mount Shasta (California, USA): Long associated with legends of hidden cities (Telos, Lemurian myths). Modern accounts link it to Grey activity, subterranean chambers, and portals between dimensions.
- Cappadocia (Turkey): Ancient underground cities such as Derinkuyu and Kaymakli could house tens of thousands. While archaeologists interpret them as refuges, traditions suggest they were custodial vaults— later repurposed by Greys as subterranean laboratories.

These bases are not isolated. They form a global network of custodianship, preserving forbidden technologies and enabling the Greys' genetic agenda.

Abduction Accounts: Echoes of Genesis 6

Modern abduction narratives describe procedures that mirror the corruption of Genesis 6:

- Genetic Sampling: Extraction of eggs, sperm, and DNA—echoing the Watchers' intrusion into human reproduction.
- Implantation: Insertion of devices or embryos, creating hybrid offspring.
- Hybridization: Breeding programs designed to produce beings neither fully human nor fully alien—just as the Nephilim were neither fully angelic nor fully human.
- Observation: Generational monitoring of abductees, suggesting long-term manipulation of bloodlines.

These accounts are not random dreams or delusions. They are ritual reenactments of Genesis 6, updated with modern technology but driven by the same ancient goal: to corrupt flesh.

The Goal: Corruption of Flesh

The Watchers' project was never about enlightenment. It was about estrangement. Their goal remains unchanged:
- To Corrupt Flesh: Creating hybrids that sever humanity from the image of GOD.
- To Confound Lineage: Blurring the boundaries of human identity and covenantal inheritance.
- To Control Reproduction: Making humanity dependent on external manipulation for survival.
- To Create Counterfeit Lineages: Establishing bloodlines loyal to estrangement, not covenant.

The Greys are the custodians of this project. Their subterranean bases are laboratories of corruption, where the serpent's legacy is preserved and advanced.

Subterranean Custodians as Guardians of Forbidden Knowledge

The Greys function as custodians—guardians of forbidden archives and technologies. Their subterranean bases preserve:
- Genetic Archives: DNA samples from abductees, stored for hybridization.
- Technological Relics: Devices derived from Watcher knowledge, reverse-engineered by human collaborators.
- Hybrid Embryos: Preserved in vats, awaiting implantation.

- Occult Rituals: Practices that blur the line between science and sorcery.

These custodians are not passive. They are active stewards of estrangement, ensuring that the corruption of flesh continues across generations.

The Military-Industrial Complex and Custodial Collaboration

Reports of underground bases often describe joint operations between Greys and human authorities. Whether through deception or collaboration, the military-industrial complex has become entangled in custodial agendas:
- Technology Exchange: Advanced technologies allegedly traded for access to human subjects.
- Secrecy Protocols: Abductions covered up, witnesses silenced, archives classified.
- Hybrid Programs: Human scientists assisting in genetic experiments, knowingly or unknowingly.
- False Disclosure: Preparing humanity to accept Greys as extraterrestrial saviors, rather than demons in engineered flesh.

The custodianship of the Greys is not only subterranean. It is systemic, infiltrating the very structures of power.

The Custodians and the Continuity of Estrangement

The subterranean custodians represent continuity. From Genesis 6 to modern abductions, the goal has remained the same: to corrupt flesh, to sever covenant, to create a lineage estranged from GOD.

The Flood erased the bodies of the Nephilim, but their spirits endured.

The Greys provide new bodies. The underground bases provide new laboratories. The abductions provide new victims. The project continues, hidden beneath mountains, mesas, and ancient cities.

Resistance to the Custodians

To resist the subterranean custodians is to remember:
- Discernment: Recognizing that abductions are not alien encounters, but demonic manipulations.
- Covenant: Preserving divine lineage against counterfeit hybridization.
- Exposure: Revealing the true nature of underground bases as custodial vaults of estrangement.
- Authority: Exercising spiritual authority over demons, regardless of their engineered forms.

The custodians may preserve forbidden knowledge, but they cannot erase covenantal memory. Their deception thrives in secrecy; resistance thrives in remembrance.

Chapter 14 –
The Ambiguity Strategy

"The fair folk are seen and unseen, believed and doubted."
— Irish proverb

The Greys' greatest weapon is ambiguity. Sightings are frequent but inconsistent, evidence is elusive. They exist in the twilight space between belief and disbelief. This mirrors the serpent's whisper and the Watchers' teachings: reveal enough to corrupt, never enough to convict. Ambiguity destabilizes, erodes trust, and severs remembrance.

Not Force But Ambiguity

The serpent's first tactic was not force, but ambiguity. In Eden, the whisper was not a denial but a question: "Yea, hath GOD said...?" It destabilized certainty, introduced doubt, and fractured remembrance. The Watchers employed the same strategy: revealing fragments of forbidden knowledge, never enough to convict, always enough to corrupt.

In the modern age, the Greys have perfected this tactic. Their greatest weapon is not technology, nor even abduction... it is ambiguity. Sightings are frequent but inconsistent. Evidence is elusive, always just beyond verification. They exist in the twilight space between belief and disbelief, between myth and science, between ridicule and revelation.

Ambiguity destabilizes. It erodes trust in institutions, divides communities, and severs remembrance of covenantal truth. It is the serpent's whisper, updated for the modern world.

The Nature of Ambiguity

Ambiguity is not absence—it is strategic uncertainty. It thrives in the space between clarity and denial. Its effects include:
- Destabilization: Creating confusion, preventing decisive action.
- Division: Splitting communities into believers and skeptics.
- Distraction: Consuming attention with endless debate.
- Erosion: Undermining trust in memory, testimony, and covenant.

Ambiguity is not weakness, it is weaponization. It ensures that the phenomenon is always present, but never provable; always disruptive, but never resolvable.

Ambiguity in Grey Encounters

The Greys' presence is marked by ambiguity:
- Sightings: Lights in the sky, craft on radar, beings glimpsed in the night—always frequent, never consistent.
- Evidence: Implants that vanish, photographs that blur, testimonies that contradict.
- Encounters: Abductions recalled in fragments, memories suppressed or distorted.
- Disclosure: Governments releasing files that confirm mystery but deny certainty.

This ambiguity is not accidental. It is engineered. It ensures that the Greys remain in the liminal space... believable enough to corrupt, deniable enough to dismiss.

The Serpent's Whisper Revisited

The ambiguity strategy mirrors the serpent's whisper in Eden:
- Partial Revelation: The serpent quoted GOD's words, but twisted them.
- Strategic Doubt: The question destabilized Eve's certainty.
- Corruption Through Uncertainty: The ambiguity opened the door to disobedience.

The Greys employ the same tactic. They reveal enough to corrupt belief, but never enough to convict themselves. They whisper through sightings, abductions, and disclosures, destabilizing remembrance.

The Watchers' Teachings

The Watchers taught forbidden arts in fragments:
- Azazel: Weapons and adornments.
- Semjaza: Enchantments and sorcery.
- Others: Astronomy, root-cutting, and signs of the heavens.

They revealed enough to corrupt humanity, but never enough to empower it fully. Their teachings destabilized, eroded trust in covenant, and severed remembrance of divine order.

The Greys continue this legacy. Their ambiguity is the modern form of the Watchers' partial revelations.

Ambiguity as Psychological Warfare

Ambiguity is not only spiritual, it is psychological. Its effects include:
- Cognitive Dissonance: Holding contradictory beliefs, unable to resolve them.
- Paralysis: Inability to act decisively, trapped in uncertainty.
- Isolation: Abductees dismissed as delusional, believers ridiculed, skeptics hardened.
- Erosion of Trust: Institutions discredited, testimonies doubted, archives dismissed.

Ambiguity is a form of psychological warfare. It destabilizes not by force, but by uncertainty.

Ambiguity and the Erosion of Remembrance

Remembrance requires clarity. Covenant is preserved through testimony, archives, and tradition. Ambiguity severs remembrance by:

- Obscuring Testimony: Making witnesses unreliable.
- Confusing Archives: Flooding records with contradictions.
- Dividing Communities: Splitting believers and skeptics.
- Undermining Covenant: Casting doubt on divine memory itself.

Ambiguity is not neutral. It is corrosive. It erodes the very foundations of remembrance.

Ambiguity in Modern Institutions

The ambiguity strategy has infiltrated modern institutions:

- Governments: Releasing files that confirm mystery but deny certainty.
- Media: Amplifying sightings but mocking belief.
- Academia: Studying phenomena but refusing conclusions.
- Religion: Divided between dismissal and obsession.

The result is paralysis. Humanity debates endlessly, but never resolves. The Greys thrive in this liminal space.

The Ambiguity Strategy as Counterfeit Revelation

Revelation is clarity… GOD's word revealed, covenant remembered. Ambiguity is counterfeit revelation… partial truths, twisted testimonies, endless uncertainty.

The Greys' ambiguity strategy is designed to replace revelation with confusion. It ensures that humanity is always seeking, never finding; always debating, never remembering.

Resistance to Ambiguity

To resist ambiguity is to reclaim remembrance:
- Discernment: Recognizing ambiguity as strategy, not accident.
- Clarity: Preserving testimony, archives, and covenantal truth.
- Unity: Refusing division between believers and skeptics, focusing on remembrance.
- Revelation: Returning to divine clarity, rejecting counterfeit ambiguity.

The serpent's whisper can be silenced. The Watchers' teachings can be discerned. The Greys' ambiguity can be resisted… through remembrance, covenant, and truth.

Chapter 15 –
Chemtrails and the Sky Grid

"The sky itself was veiled with smoke and dust."
— Pliny the Younger, on Vesuvius

Persistent contrails form grids across the sky. Once officially called condensation, but now there are many within the government who have come forward with the truth.

Precedents exist: Operation Sea-Spray, Operation LAC, UK MoD dispersals. Hypotheses abound: weather modification, geoengineering, population control, electromagnetic grids. The sky has become a canvas of control, echoing the Watchers' manipulation of the firmament.

Now the facts are coming out as government agencies are admitting to funding these programs. Are there ulterior motives to reduce birthrates and populations and what are their known dangers?

108

Not Just Condensation

The sky has always been a canvas of meaning. In antiquity, the Watchers taught humanity to read the stars, to manipulate the firmament, and to corrupt the order of creation. Today, the sky has once again become a canvas... not of covenant, but of control.

Persistent contrails, once dismissed as harmless condensation, now form grids across the sky. Their patterns are too deliberate, their persistence too unnatural, to be explained away as mere exhaust. For decades, governments denied the phenomenon. Yet whistleblowers, declassified documents, and official admissions of geoengineering research have begun to reveal a deeper truth: the Sky Grid is real.

The ambiguity of chemtrails mirrors the serpent's whisper: reveal enough to corrupt, never enough to convict. The result is confusion, division, and erosion of trust. But the pattern is clear: the manipulation of the heavens continues, echoing the Watchers' ancient strategy of estrangement.

Persistent Contrails and the Sky Grid

Contrails (condensation trails left by aircraft) were once fleeting, dissipating within minutes. But since the late 20th century, observers have noted persistent trails that linger for hours, spreading into artificial cloud cover. These trails often form grids, X-patterns, and lattices, covering entire regions.

The official explanation (variations in humidity and temperature) fails to account for the deliberate geometry, the persistence, and the correlation with weather anomalies. The Sky Grid is not random. It is structured, intentional, and global.

Historical Precedents of Atmospheric Experimentation

The idea of dispersing substances into the atmosphere is not speculative, it has precedent:

- Operation Sea-Spray (1950, San Francisco): The U.S. Navy released Serratia marcescens bacteria over the city to test biological dispersal.
- Operation LAC (Large Area Coverage, 1957–58): The U.S. Army dispersed zinc cadmium sulfide over large swaths of the Midwest to study aerosol spread.
- UK Ministry of Defence Dispersals (1940s–1970s): The MoD admitted to releasing bacteria and chemicals over populated areas to test vulnerability.

These programs prove that governments have experimented with atmospheric dispersal on civilian populations... without their consent. The Sky Grid is not without precedent. It is the continuation of a pattern.

Hypotheses of Purpose

The Sky Grid has been linked to multiple hypotheses, each echoing the Watchers' manipulation of the firmament:

1. Weather Modification
   - Cloud seeding and atmospheric manipulation to control rainfall, drought, or storms.
   - Strategic use in agriculture, warfare, or disaster management.
2. Geoengineering
   - Solar radiation management: dispersing reflective particles to cool the planet.

- Officially discussed in climate change mitigation programs.
3. Population Control
    - Hypotheses suggest dispersal of chemicals to reduce fertility, weaken immunity, or increase dependency.
    - Echoes of ancient attempts to corrupt flesh and sever covenantal lineage.
4. Electromagnetic Grids
    - Metallic particulates creating conductive layers in the atmosphere.
    - Potential use in conjunction with HAARP-like technologies for communication, surveillance, or mind-influence.

Each hypothesis reflects a different facet of control. Together, they form a picture of the Sky Grid as a canvas of estrangement.

Admissions and Funding

For decades, officials dismissed chemtrails as conspiracy. Yet in recent years, agencies have admitted to funding geoengineering research:
- U.S. National Academy of Sciences (2015): Published reports on solar radiation management and carbon dioxide removal.
- Harvard's Solar Geoengineering Research Program: Funded studies on stratospheric aerosol injection.
- UK Royal Society (2009): Released reports on geoengineering as a climate intervention.

These admissions confirm that governments are exploring atmospheric manipulation. The line between research and deployment remains ambiguous... by design.

The Ambiguity Strategy in the Sky

The Sky Grid thrives on ambiguity:
- Visible but Denied: Trails are seen daily, yet dismissed as condensation.
- Admitted but Minimized: Geoengineering research acknowledged, but framed as hypothetical.
- Discussed but Discredited: Whistleblowers ridiculed, evidence fragmented.

This ambiguity mirrors the serpent's whisper and the Watchers' teachings: reveal enough to corrupt, never enough to convict. The result is confusion, division, and erosion of trust in both institutions and memory.

Ulterior Motives: Population and Birthrates

Are there ulterior motives behind the Sky Grid? Some hypotheses suggest:
- Fertility Reduction: Aerosols containing endocrine disruptors or heavy metals could reduce birthrates.
- Immune Suppression: Chronic exposure weakening populations, increasing dependency on pharmaceuticals.
- Behavioral Influence: Atmospheric particulates interacting with electromagnetic fields to affect mood or cognition.

While definitive proof remains elusive, the pattern echoes Genesis 6: the corruption of flesh, the manipulation of lineage, the severing of covenantal inheritance.

Known Dangers of Aerosol Programs

Even official geoengineering proposals admit risks:
- Ozone Depletion: Aerosols could damage the protective ozone layer.
- Weather Disruption: Altered rainfall patterns, droughts, and floods.
- Soil and Water Contamination: Accumulation of metals and particulates.
- Health Effects: Respiratory illness, cardiovascular stress, neurological impact.
- Termination Shock: Sudden cessation of geoengineering could trigger catastrophic warming.

These dangers are not speculative. They are acknowledged in scientific literature. The Sky Grid is not without cost.

The Sky as a Canvas of Control

The Watchers once manipulated the firmament, teaching forbidden astronomy and corrupting humanity's relationship with the heavens. Today, the Sky Grid echoes that manipulation. The heavens, once a testimony of covenant, have become a canvas of control.

The trails that crisscross the sky are not only physical. They are symbolic. They represent the erasure of remembrance, the corruption of creation, and the imposition of estrangement.

Resistance and Remembrance

To resist the Sky Grid is to remember:
- Discernment: Recognizing the ambiguity strategy as intentional.
- Exposure: Documenting, archiving, and testifying to the phenomenon.
- Covenant: Preserving trust in divine order, even as the firmament is manipulated.
- Accountability: Demanding transparency from institutions that fund or deploy atmospheric programs.

The Sky Grid may cover the heavens, but it cannot erase covenantal memory. The heavens still declare the glory of GOD, even when veiled by grids of control.

Chapter 16 –
Vaccines, mRNA, and the Flesh

"What is bred of gods and men is neither mortal nor divine."
— *Pindar, Nemean Odes*

Has vaccination really saved lives? Certainly abuses exist: Tuskegee, Guatemala, MK-ULTRA. mRNA technology rewrites cellular instructions, echoing Genesis 6's corruption of flesh. Transhumanist ambitions risk repeating the Watchers' sin: to be "as gods" by altering creation itself.

The New mRNA Frontier

Humanity has always sought to preserve life against the threat of disease. Vaccination, hailed as one of the greatest medical achievements, has been credited with saving millions of lives. Yet the story is not simple. Alongside genuine advances, there exists a shadow history of abuse, coercion, and manipulation. From Tuskegee to Guatemala, from MK-ULTRA to covert testing programs, the record shows that medicine has often been weaponized against the very populations it claimed to protect.

Now, in the 21st century, a new frontier has emerged: mRNA technology. Unlike traditional vaccines, which introduce weakened or inactivated pathogens, mRNA vaccines deliver genetic instructions, programming the body's cells to produce proteins they would not otherwise create. This is not merely medicine... it is rewriting the flesh.

The theological implications are profound. Genesis 6 describes the corruption of flesh by the Watchers, who sought to alter creation itself. Today, transhumanist ambitions echo that sin: to be "as gods" by rewriting the code of life. The danger is not only medical but spiritual. If humanity is made in the image of GOD, then altering that image risks estrangement... transforming man into something else, something beast-like, no longer bearing the divine imprint.

This chapter examines the ambiguity of vaccines, the abuses of the past, the rise of mRNA technology, and the possibility that the Watchers' ancient project continues... through the manipulation of flesh in the name of science and progress.

Vaccination: Between Healing and Control

Vaccination has been credited with eradicating smallpox, reducing polio, and controlling measles. Yet the narrative is double-edged:

- Healing: Millions of lives saved, diseases curtailed.
- Control: Mandates, coercion, and forced inoculations.
- Exploitation: Experiments on vulnerable populations.
- Profit: Pharmaceutical monopolies built on patents.
- Suppression: Alternative treatments dismissed or censored.

The question is not whether vaccines have saved lives—they have. The question is whether vaccination has also been used as a tool of control, a means of manipulating populations under the guise of health.

Historical Abuses: The Shadow Record

The history of medical experimentation reveals a pattern of betrayal:

- Tuskegee Syphilis Study (1932–1972): African American men were denied treatment for syphilis so researchers could study the disease's progression.
- Guatemala Experiments (1946–1948): U.S. researchers deliberately infected prisoners and mental patients with syphilis and gonorrhea without consent.
- MK-ULTRA (1950s–1970s): CIA program testing drugs, hypnosis, and mind control on unwitting subjects.
- Operation Sea-Spray (1950): Bacteria released over San Francisco to test dispersal.

These abuses prove that medicine and science have been weaponized before. They erode trust in institutions and raise the question: if such things were done in the past, what prevents them from being done again?

mRNA Technology: Rewriting the Flesh

mRNA vaccines represent a radical departure from tradition. Instead of introducing a pathogen, they deliver messenger RNA... genetic instructions that direct cells to produce specific proteins.

Implications include:
- Programmable Biology: Cells become factories for synthetic proteins.
- Temporary or Permanent?: Officially described as temporary, but long-term effects remain uncertain.
- Beyond Vaccines: mRNA platforms are being explored for cancer, genetic disorders, and enhancement.
- Control of Flesh: Whoever controls the code controls the body.

This is not passive medicine... it is engineering. It echoes the Watchers' corruption of flesh in Genesis 6, where forbidden knowledge altered creation itself.

Transhumanism: The Dream of Being "As Gods"

The transhumanist movement openly aspires to transcend humanity:
- Genetic Enhancement: Editing DNA to eliminate disease or enhance traits.
- Cybernetic Integration: Merging flesh with machines.

- Immortality Projects: Uploading consciousness or extending life indefinitely.
- Redefinition of Humanity: Creating beings no longer fully human.

These ambitions echo the serpent's promise in Eden: "Ye shall be as gods." They are not new. They are the continuation of the Watchers' sin. To alter creation is to usurp the Creator. To rewrite flesh is to risk erasing the image of GOD.

The Beast System and the Image of Man

Revelation describes a Beast system, where humanity is marked, controlled, and estranged from GOD. The corruption of flesh may be part of this system:
- From Image to Beast: Humanity, made in GOD's image, altered into something else.
- Estrangement: Separation from covenant through genetic manipulation.
- Control: Populations managed through biotechnology and digital identity systems.
- Counterfeit Covenant: A new "mark" replacing divine remembrance.

The danger is not only physical but spiritual. If humanity ceases to bear GOD's image, it ceases to be human in the covenantal sense. It becomes beast-like, estranged, and enslaved.

The Watchers' Project Continued

Genesis 6 describes the Watchers corrupting flesh through hybridization. Today, mRNA technology and transhumanist ambitions may represent the continuation of that project:

- Hybridization: Blending human DNA with synthetic or non-human code.
- Corruption: Altering the body's natural design.
- Estrangement: Severing humanity from GOD's image.
- Control: Establishing a Beast system of surveillance and manipulation.

The Watchers' sin was not only rebellion, it was engineering. Their goal was to alter creation. That goal may be alive today, hidden beneath the language of science and progress.

Resistance and Remembrance

To resist is not to reject all medicine, but:
- Discernment: Recognizing when technology crosses from healing to corruption.
- Remembrance: Preserving the truth that humanity is made in GOD's image.
- Accountability: Demanding transparency from institutions that manipulate flesh.
- Covenant: Trusting in divine design, not counterfeit enhancements.

The serpent's whisper continues: "Ye shall be as gods." But remembrance silences the whisper. Humanity is already made in GOD's image. To alter that image is not progress. It is estrangement.

Chapter 17 –
Food, Additives, and Pesticides

"Poison is in everything, and nothing is without poison."
— *Paracelsus*

Modern diets are saturated with additives and pesticides: aspartame, MSG, glyphosate. Long-term effects remain debated. Biblical dietary laws were protective, distinguishing clean from unclean. Modern food corruption echoes the serpent's tactic: altering what was once pure.

Food is Covenantal

Food is covenantal. It is how creation nourishes the creature, how the gifts of the earth become strength, clarity, and remembrance. When the diet of a people is corrupted, their memory fades, their vigor dulls, their discernment erodes. The modern food system... industrialized, chemically engineered, shelf-life optimized... has turned nourishment into commodity, and commodity into control.

This chapter traces the architecture of ingestion... how additives, pesticides, and processing conspire to weaken the body and cloud the mind. It shows how convenience and profit reshape appetite, how packaging spawns endocrine disruption, and how "modern medicine" becomes the permanent crutch for harms engineered upstream. It ties this to the Watchers' plan to estrange humanity from covenant by corrupting flesh, shortening lifespans, and driving dependence on systems that serve control rather than health.

The industrialization of appetite

The modern food chain emphasizes speed, stability, and scale over true nourishment. Yield replaces diversity; shelf life replaces freshness; uniformity replaces seasonality. This system is optimized to meet logistics, not to honor life.

- Commodity monocultures: Vast acreages of corn, soy, and wheat feed processed products, livestock confined feeding operations, and industrial oils—while biodiversity collapses.
- Ultra-processing: Fractionation, extrusion, hydrogenation, and recombination turn crops into

"edible food-like substances" with altered textures, flavors, and metabolic effects.
- Flavor engineering: Synthetic flavors and enhancers mask nutrient poverty, training palates to prefer the engineered over the earthly.
- Shelf stability over vitality: Pasteurization, irradiation, and preservatives prioritize longevity and transportability at the cost of micronutrients and enzymes.

This is not simply modernization. It is the inversion of nourishment. A people fed by machines begin to resemble their feed: uniform, compliant, and dependent.

Additives that alter biology

Additives are introduced to stabilize, color, emulsify, sweeten, and preserve... but their biological consequences are broad and cumulative.

Here are several major examples:
- Sweeteners and appetite signaling
- High-fructose corn syrup: Overloads hepatic metabolism, promotes de novo lipogenesis, elevates triglycerides, and contributes to insulin resistance.
- Artificial sweeteners (e.g., aspartame, sucralose): Disrupt gut microbiota, alter insulin response, and decouple sweetness from caloric content, confusing satiety pathways.
- Industrial seed oils and oxidative stress
- Omega-6 heavy oils (soybean, corn, sunflower, canola): Prone to oxidation and aldehyde formation at heat;

skew omega-6/omega-3 balance toward chronic inflammation.

- Partially hydrogenated trans fats (now phased out in many regions): Alter membrane fluidity, increase LDL, decrease HDL, and disrupt endothelial function.
- Emulsifiers and gut barrier integrity
- Polysorbate 80, carboxymethylcellulose: Associated with mucosal erosion, increased intestinal permeability ("leaky gut"), and microbiome dysbiosis—priming systemic inflammation.
- Carrageenan: Linked to gastrointestinal irritation and altered immune signaling in susceptible individuals.
- Preservatives and nitrosative stress
- Nitrites/nitrates (in processed meats): Under certain conditions form nitrosamines, compounds associated with cancer risk.
- BHA/BHT: Antioxidants in fat-containing foods; controversial for endocrine and carcinogenic potential depending on dose and context.
- Artificial colors and neurobehavioral effects
- Synthetic dyes (Red 40, Yellow 5): Correlated in some studies with hyperactivity and attention issues in sensitive children; labeling or restrictions apply in parts of the world.
- Thickeners, gelling agents, and satiety distortion
- Modified starches, gums (xanthan, guar): Safe in moderation, but at scale can distort texture cues, enabling overconsumption of calorie-dense products without natural satiety.

These ingredients shape hormones, metabolism, and the microbiome (also known as the "second brain") altering mood, cognition, and immune calibration. Appetite becomes algorithm; biology becomes throughput.

Pesticides, herbicides, and the invisible diet

Chemical agriculture saturates soils, crops, and water with compounds designed to kill. Residues enter bodies daily, often at low doses that evade acute toxicity but amplify chronic risk.

- Organophosphates: Acetylcholinesterase inhibitors; chronic exposure linked to neurodevelopmental delays and behavioral changes. Sublethal doses matter in cumulative, prenatal, and early-life contexts.
- Neonicotinoids: Nicotinic receptor agonists; ecologically devastating to pollinators; questions remain about low-dose neurological effects in humans.
- Glyphosate and adjuvants: Widely used herbicide; debates persist on carcinogenicity, endocrine effects, and microbiome disruption; adjuvants can alter absorption and toxicity profiles.
- Fungicides (azoles, strobilurins): Interact with cytochrome P450 enzymes, potentially modulating steroidogenesis and detox pathways.
- Post-harvest treatments: Anti-sprouting agents and fumigants extend storage but add chemical layers to staples.

The cumulative load (small doses across years) reshapes endocrine tone, immune vigilance, and neurocognitive trajectories. What enters the soil enters the self.

Packaging, contact materials, and endocrine drift

Beyond food and field, packaging and contact materials become vectors of invasion:

- Plasticizers (phthalates): Migrate into fatty foods; associated with reduced testosterone, altered reproductive outcomes, and metabolic risk.
- Bisphenols (e.g., BPA, BPS): Estrogenic activity; linked to insulin resistance, thyroid interference, and developmental effects.
- Per- and polyfluoroalkyl substances (PFAS): "Forever chemicals" in nonstick, grease-proof packaging; bioaccumulative, associated with immune and lipid dysregulation.

Endocrine rhythm is the orchestra of the body; these compounds introduce static, detuning the score.

The symptomatology of estrangement

When nourishment becomes throughput, the body remembers the assault:

- Metabolic dysregulation: Insulin resistance, fatty liver, visceral adiposity—energy abundance coupled with cellular scarcity.
- Neurocognitive erosion: Brain fog, mood lability, attention deficits—microbiome-brain axis strained by additives and residues.
- Immune confusion: Allergies, autoimmunity, chronic low-grade inflammation—barrier integrity compromised, danger signals ubiquitous.

- Reproductive drift: Altered puberty timing, reduced fertility indicators, endocrine tone skewed by exogenous mimics.
- Longevity contraction: Lifespan and health span pressured by chronic disease onset and polypharmacy dependence.

A body under such load leans on medicine... not for healing root causes, but for symptomatic management. Dependency becomes design.

Convenience, compliance, and the hospital supply chain

The architecture of control begins far upstream:
- Hyper-palatable design: Foods engineered to overwhelm satiety, increase frequency, and habituate to additives.
- Marketing to vulnerable populations: Children targeted with colors, mascots, and rewards; lower-income communities saturated with ultra-processed options.
- Food deserts and time scarcity: Structural barriers push households toward convenience calories; the system rewards shelf life, not vitality.
- Clinical capture: Chronic conditions funneled into lifelong medication regimens; food harms normalized, pharmaceutical fixes valorized.

Thus the loop closes: the diet generates disease; the disease sustains markets; the markets sustain the diet.

The Watchers' plan: corrupt flesh, cloud mind, shorten days

In Genesis, the Watchers corrupted flesh and taught estranging arts. The modern food matrix is their secular liturgy:
- Corrupt the flesh: Alter membranes, hormones, and microbiota; weaken defenses; inflame tissues.
- Cloud the mind: Disrupt neurotransmission and gut-brain signaling; seed apathy, anxiety, and distraction.
- Shorten the days: Advance onset of chronic disease; compress healthspan; accelerate frailty.
- Bind to the system: Require permanent maintenance through industrial medicine; normalize managed decline.

This is not simply poor diet, it is engineered estrangement: a people less resilient, less clear, and more compliant.

Paths of remembrance and resilience

Without offering medical advice, strategic pivots can reduce upstream load and restore agency:
- Whole food priority: Emphasize minimally processed, diverse plants and responsibly raised proteins; favor seasonality over shelf life.
- Fat quality shift: Replace omega-6-heavy seed oils with monounsaturated and balanced sources (e.g., olive oil); include omega-3s (e.g., fatty fish) to recalibrate inflammation.
- Additive awareness: Limit products with long ingredient lists; avoid emulsifier-heavy, dye-heavy items where feasible.

- Residue reduction: Wash produce, peel when appropriate, consider sourcing with lower pesticide footprints.
- Packaging prudence: Prefer glass or stainless contact for hot/fatty foods; reduce reliance on nonstick and grease-proof wrappers.
- Microbiome friendly: Include fermented foods and diverse fibers; reduce sweetener reliance to support gut-brain harmony.
- Local supply webs: Support producers who prioritize soil health, biodiversity, and transparency; rebuild trust at the source.

These are acts of remembrance... small covenants in kitchens and communities that push back against systemic estrangement.

The covenant of the table

Every meal is a liturgy. The table can be a site of control, or a site of covenant. When food honors creation, the body honors its Maker. When appetite is retrained toward truth, the mind clears, the immune chorus reorients, and the household steps out of dependency into stewardship.

This is resistance as remembrance: the daily refusal to let engineered consumption define human destiny.

Chapter 18 –
The Mandela Effect and Reality Shifts

"Time is a moving image of eternity."
— Plato, Timaeus

Collective different memories (Nelson Mandela's death, Berenstain vs. Berenstein Bears, Star Wars misquotes, and many more) suggest manipulation of memory or even reality. Explanations range from psychology to quantum shifts to deliberate tampering. Amos 8:11–12 warns of a famine of truth. If memory itself can be altered, remembrance is severed. Or has reality itself been altered?

Memory or Reality Shifts?

Memory is the foundation of identity. Without remembrance, covenant collapses. Without continuity, truth dissolves. In recent years, a strange phenomenon has unsettled millions: the Mandela Effect... collective memories of events, names, or details that differ from the historical record.

There are too many discrepancies to cover here. Some include: Did Nelson Mandela die in prison in the 1980s, or live until 2013? Was it Berenstain Bears or Berenstein Bears? Did Darth Vader say, "Luke, I am your father" or "No, I am your father"? These discrepancies, trivial on the surface, have profound implications.

Are they mere psychological quirks, or evidence of reality shifts?

This chapter explores the Mandela Effect as a symptom of estrangement. It considers explanations from psychology, quantum physics, and technological tampering. It ties the phenomenon to the Watchers' ancient strategy: to confuse, disorient, and sever remembrance. If memory itself can be altered, then the famine of truth Amos warned of is not future, it is present.

The Mandela Effect: Defining the Phenomenon

The term "Mandela Effect" was coined in 2009 by researcher Fiona Broome, who discovered that many people shared her "false memory" of Nelson Mandela dying in prison in the 1980s.

Since then, countless examples have emerged and here are some:
    • Names and Spellings

- Berenstain Bears vs. Berenstein Bears
- Febreze vs. Febreeze
- Oscar Mayer vs. Oscar Meyer
- "Luke, I am your father" vs. "No, I am your father" (Star Wars)
- "Mirror, mirror on the wall" vs. "Magic mirror on the wall" (Snow White)
- "Life is like a box of chocolates" vs. "Life was like a box of chocolates" (Forrest Gump)
- Logos and Brands
- Monopoly Man with or without a monocle
- Fruit of the Loom logo with or without a cornucopia
- KitKat with or without a hyphen

These discrepancies are often dismissed as faulty memory. Yet the sheer scale and consistency of shared false memories suggest something much deeper.

Psychological Explanations?

Mainstream psychology attempts to offer several explanations:
- Confabulation: The brain fills gaps in memory with plausible details.
- Schema Theory: Memory is reconstructed based on patterns and expectations.
- Social Reinforcement: False memories spread through repetition and group affirmation.
- Misinformation Effect: Exposure to incorrect information alters recall.

These mechanisms are real. Yet they do not fully explain the persistence, scale, and emotional conviction of Mandela Effect memories. Millions are not merely misremembering, they are certain of these changes.

Quantum and Multiverse Hypotheses

Some propose that the Mandela Effect reflects quantum shifts or multiverse bleed-throughs:

- Parallel Realities: Slightly different timelines converging, leaving residue in memory.
- Quantum Decoherence: Observers collapsing different histories into shared confusion.
- Dimensional Overlap: Boundaries between realities thinning, producing anomalies.

While speculative, these theories resonate with the sense that reality itself is unstable... that memory is not merely faulty, but fractured.

Technological Tampering: The Watchers' Hand?

Another hypothesis is deliberate manipulation. Could advanced technology alter records, archives, or even memory itself?

- Hadron Collider (CERN): Popular speculation links high-energy particle collisions to reality shifts, though no evidence confirms this.
- Digital Archives: In an age where most memory is stored digitally, subtle edits could rewrite history without detection.
- Electromagnetic Manipulation: Technologies capable of influencing perception or memory at scale.
- Watcher-Directed Influence: Ancient powers using modern tools to continue their project of estrangement.

If the Watchers once corrupted flesh, could they now corrupt memory? If remembrance is severed, covenant collapses. Confusion becomes control.

The Plot of Confusion

The Mandela Effect, whether psychological, quantum, or technological, serves a single purpose: confusion. Confusion leads to:

- Disorientation: If memory cannot be trusted, what can?
- Division: Believers and skeptics argue, eroding unity.
- Dependency: Populations rely on external authorities to define reality.
- Estrangement: Severed from remembrance, humanity drifts from covenant.

This is the famine of truth Amos warned of. Not a famine of bread, but of memory. Not a thirst for water, but for certainty. If memory itself can be altered, remembrance is severed. And without remembrance, covenant collapses.

Resistance Through Remembrance

To resist is to remember:

- Scripture: Anchoring memory in the Word, unchanging and eternal.
- Testimony: Preserving oral and written witness across generations.
- Discernment: Recognizing confusion as strategy, not accident.
- Community: Strengthening collective memory through shared covenant.

Chapter 19 –
The Digital Cage

"He who controls the archives controls the future."
— *French Revolution maxim*

From scrolls to screens, memory has been centralized. Today, archives are digital, subject to deletion and curation. Surveillance systems (PRISM, social credit, facial recognition) form an invisible cage. Unlike past empires, the modern empire controls data. Artificial Intelligence is part of this. What are the Watchers up to, and how could this fit into their plan to manipulate mankind?

From Clay Scrolls to Digital Data

From clay tablets to scrolls, from codices to printed books, humanity's memory has always been preserved in tangible form. Archives were dispersed, libraries scattered across empires, and knowledge (though vulnerable to fire and conquest) remained decentralized. But in the modern age, memory has been centralized. From scroll to screen, the archive has become digital.

Today, the vast majority of human knowledge, communication, and testimony exists not in stone or parchment, but in servers, clouds, and databases. These archives are subject to deletion, curation, and manipulation. What is remembered can be erased; what is erased can be forgotten. The digital archive is not immutable, it is malleable.

Surveillance systems (PRISM, social credit scoring, facial recognition, biometric IDs) form an invisible cage. Unlike past empires, which controlled territory, the modern empire controls data. And unlike past tyrannies, which relied on visible force, the modern empire relies on invisible algorithms.

Artificial Intelligence is the newest custodian of this cage. It sorts, filters, predicts, and polices. It is not neutral. It is a tool of control. The question is: what are the Watchers up to? How does this digital cage fit into their ancient plan to manipulate mankind?

From Scroll to Screen: The Centralization of Memory

The shift is profound. A burned library destroys a city's memory. A deleted server erases the world's. The digital archive is both vast and fragile, both eternal and ephemeral. It is the perfect tool for control.

- Ancient Archives: Clay tablets in Mesopotamia, papyrus scrolls in Egypt, codices in Rome—knowledge was dispersed, fragile, but plural.
- Libraries of Antiquity: The Library of Alexandria sought to centralize, but its destruction proved the fragility of concentration.
- The Printing Press: Decentralized knowledge again, empowering reformations and revolutions.
- The Digital Archive: Today, memory is centralized in servers owned by corporations and states.

The Architecture of the Digital Cage

The cage is invisible, but its bars are real:
- PRISM (NSA Program): Mass collection of digital communications, revealed in 2013, showing the scale of surveillance.
- Social Credit Systems (China): Scores assigned to citizens based on behavior, purchases, and associations, determining access to services.
- Facial Recognition: Cameras in public spaces, airports, and streets, identifying and tracking individuals in real time.
- Biometric IDs: Fingerprints, iris scans, and DNA profiles linked to financial and governmental systems.
- Algorithmic Policing: Predictive models directing law enforcement, often opaque and biased.

This is not the cage of iron bars, it is the cage of invisible data. It does not confine the body; it confines the possibility of action. It shapes behavior through surveillance, nudging, and fear of exclusion.

Artificial Intelligence: The Custodian of Control

AI (Artificial Intelligence) is not merely a tool, it is the custodian of the digital cage:
- Curation: Deciding what information is seen, what is hidden, what is amplified.
- Prediction: Anticipating behavior, purchases, and even dissent.
- Policing: Flagging "misinformation," monitoring speech, enforcing compliance.
- Replacement: Automating jobs, decisions, and even creativity, reducing human agency.

AI is the Watchers' dream: a system that can manipulate without revealing itself, that can control without appearing to coerce. It is the whisper of the serpent, encoded in code.

The Watchers' Plan: Manipulation Through Data

The Watchers once corrupted flesh. Now they corrupt memory. Their plan is consistent:
- Confusion: Flooding the digital archive with contradictions, eroding trust.
- Control: Using surveillance to enforce compliance, shaping behavior through fear.
- Estrangement: Severing humanity from remembrance, replacing covenant with algorithm.
- Counterfeit Omniscience: Presenting the digital cage as all-seeing, all-knowing, a counterfeit of divine omniscience.

The digital cage is not merely political, it is spiritual. It is the Watchers' attempt to replace GOD's omniscience with their own counterfeit system of surveillance and control.

The Famine of Truth

Amos warned of a famine, not of bread, but of truth. The digital cage helps create this famine:

- Censorship: Voices silenced, archives deleted.
- Revision: Histories rewritten, records altered.
- Flooding: Truth drowned in noise, misinformation, and distraction.
- Dependency: Populations reliant on curated feeds for reality itself.

When memory is digital, it is editable. When truth is editable, it is severed. When remembrance is severed, covenant collapses.

Resistance to the Digital Cage

To resist is to remember:

- Decentralization: Preserving physical archives, books, and testimonies.
- Transparency: Demanding accountability in algorithms and surveillance.
- Community: Strengthening oral and local memory, beyond digital systems.
- Covenant: Anchoring truth in the Word of GOD, unchanging and eternal.

The cage is invisible, but it is not invincible. Remembrance is resistance. Covenant is freedom.

Chapter 20 – The Financial Net

"Money is the sinews of war."
— *Cicero*

Money has shifted from gold and silver to fiat and to code. SWIFT, credit cards, blockchain, CBDCs... each step centralizes control. Programmable money enforces compliance. This is the financial equivalent of the Watchers' Table: a system of control disguised as convenience.

About Money

Money is not neutral. It is the bloodstream of civilization, the medium through which power flows, and the architecture by which empires rise and fall. From the gold and silver coins of antiquity to the fiat currencies of modern states, from the plastic of credit cards to the invisible digits of blockchain, money has always been more than exchange... it is control.

Today, money is no longer tangible. It is code. It is data. It is programmable. Each step in the evolution of money has centralized control further, tightening the net around humanity. SWIFT, credit cards, blockchain, and CBDCs form the lattice of a Financial Net... a system of surveillance and compliance, where access to commerce is contingent on obedience.

This is the financial equivalent of the Watchers' Table: a banquet of control disguised as convenience. The Watchers once corrupted flesh; now they corrupt exchange. Their goal is the same: estrangement from GOD, dependency on systems of control, and the replacement of covenantal freedom with counterfeit provision.

From Gold and Silver to Fiat: The First Shift

- Gold and Silver: For millennia, money was tethered to tangible value. Gold and silver coins carried intrinsic worth, recognized across cultures.
- Fiat Currency: In the 20th century, money was severed from gold. The U.S. abandoned the gold standard in 1971, and currencies became fiat—backed not by metal, but by decree.

- Implications: Fiat money allowed governments to print without restraint, fueling debt, inflation, and cycles of boom and bust. The tether to tangible value was cut; money became trust in authority.

This was the first tightening of the net: money shifted from creation to decree, from covenant to command.

SWIFT and the Global Grid

- SWIFT (Society for Worldwide Interbank Financial Telecommunication): Founded in 1973, SWIFT became the backbone of global finance, enabling banks to transfer funds across borders.
- Centralization: Though presented as neutral, SWIFT is controlled by a consortium of major banks and subject to geopolitical influence. Nations can be cut off, individuals flagged, transactions frozen.
- Weaponization: Sanctions enforced through SWIFT demonstrate that access to money is not universal—it is conditional.

SWIFT is the nervous system of the Financial Net: invisible, global, and absolute.

Credit Cards and the Plastic Leash

- Credit Expansion: Credit cards, introduced in the mid-20th century, transformed consumption. Debt became normalized, and households became perpetual borrowers.

- Surveillance: Every purchase is tracked, every transaction logged. Spending habits become data, sold to corporations and governments.
- Dependency: Credit cards create cycles of debt, interest, and dependency. The borrower is indeed servant to the lender.

Plastic was marketed as freedom, but it was a leash... tying individuals to banks, data brokers, and systems of surveillance.

Blockchain: Decentralization or Trojan Horse?

Blockchain is paradox: a tool of freedom turned into a tool of control. It is the Watchers' whisper... offering liberty, delivering bondage.

- Promise of Decentralization: Bitcoin and blockchain were heralded as liberation from central banks, offering peer-to-peer exchange beyond control.
- Reality of Surveillance: Blockchain is transparent; every transaction is permanent and traceable. Far from anonymity, it creates a ledger of total visibility.
- Institutional Adoption: Governments and corporations now explore blockchain not to decentralize, but to centralize further—using its permanence to enforce compliance.

CBDCs: The Programmable Cage

CBDCs are the tightening of the net. They are not money—they are permission slips. They are the financial equivalent of the Mark: access to commerce contingent on obedience.

- Central Bank Digital Currencies (CBDCs): Digital currencies issued directly by central banks, replacing cash with programmable money.
- Programmability: CBDCs can be coded with conditions—where, when, and how money can be spent.
- Surveillance: Every transaction is visible to the issuing authority. Privacy disappears.
- Control: Non-compliance can mean frozen accounts, expired funds, or restricted purchases.

The Watchers' Table: Control Disguised as Provision

In ancient texts, the Watchers corrupted humanity by teaching forbidden arts and demanding allegiance. Their table was not nourishment, it was control.

The Financial Net is the modern Watchers' Table:
- Disguised as Convenience: Credit cards, mobile payments, and CBDCs promise ease.
- Engineered for Dependency: Debt, inflation, and programmable money ensure reliance.
- Structured for Control: Access to commerce becomes conditional on compliance.
- Counterfeit Covenant: The system offers provision, but at the cost of freedom.

The Watchers' goal is not wealth, it is estrangement from GOD. By controlling exchange, they control allegiance.

The Beast System and the Financial Net

The Bible's book of Revelation describes a Beast system where no one can buy or sell without the mark. The Financial Net is its infrastructure:
- Global Grid: SWIFT and digital payment systems connect all nations.
- Surveillance: Every transaction tracked, every purchase logged.
- Programmability: CBDCs enforce compliance through code.
- Exclusion: Dissenters cut off from commerce, unable to buy or sell.

The Financial Net is not future, it is present and is here now. The infrastructure is here. The mark is not only physical, it is financial.

Resistance and Remembrance

To resist is to remember:
- Diversification: Preserving tangible assets (gold, silver, land) beyond digital control.
- Community Exchange: Local barter, mutual aid, and decentralized networks.
- Transparency: Exposing the mechanisms of financial control.
- Covenant: Trusting in GOD's provision, not counterfeit tables.

The Financial Net may tighten, but remembrance is freedom. The true table is not the Watchers'... it is the GOD's.

Chapter 21 –
Pharmakeia and the Spell of the Sorcerers

"For by thy sorceries were all nations deceived."
— *Revelation 18:23*

Let's discuss how pharmaceuticals, narcotics, and the ancient practice of pharmakeia tie into the Beast system of control.

Pharmakeia comes from the Greek

The Greek word pharmakeia appears in the New Testament of the Bible, often translated as "sorcery" or "witchcraft." Yet its root meaning is clear: the use of drugs, potions, and enchantments to manipulate body and mind. In antiquity, pharmakeia was not healing, it was control. It was the blending of medicine and magic, of chemistry and enchantment, of healing and harm.

Today, the pharmaceutical industry dominates global health. Pills, injections, and prescriptions are the sacraments of modern life. Yet beneath the white coats and sterile laboratories lies the same story: pharmakeia as manipulation. The Watchers once taught forbidden arts, corrupting flesh and estranging humanity from GOD. Modern pharmakeia continues this project, binding populations to lifelong dependency, clouding minds, and replacing covenantal trust with chemical control.

Even the symbols of medicine (the caduceus, the rod of Asclepius) carry ancient meanings, rooted in serpents, gods, and sorcery. These emblems are not neutral. They reveal the spiritual undercurrent of pharmakeia: the serpent entwined with healing, the counterfeit covenant of the sorcerers' table.

Pharmakeia in Scripture

The New Testament of the Bible warns repeatedly of pharmakeia:
- Galatians 5:20 — Lists pharmakeia among the "works of the flesh."
- Revelation 9:21 — Humanity refuses to repent of murders, sorceries (pharmakeia), fornication, and thefts.

- Revelation 18:23 — "By thy sorceries (pharmakeia) were all nations deceived."

Pharmakeia is not healing, it is deception. It is the use of substances to manipulate, control, and estrange. It is the counterfeit of true healing, which comes from covenant with GOD.

Ancient Pharmakeia: Potions and Enchantments

In antiquity, pharmakeia was practiced by:
- Egyptian Priests: Blending herbs, minerals, and incantations.
- Greek Sorcerers: Using potions to seduce, poison, or enchant.
- Babylonian Magi: Combining astrology, ritual, and drugs.
- Roman Physicians: Often indistinguishable from magicians, prescribing amulets and charms alongside remedies.

Pharmakeia was never neutral. It was always a double-edged sword: healing and harming, blessing and cursing, medicine and magic. It blurs the line between science and sorcery.

The Rise of Modern Pharmaceuticals

The modern pharmaceutical industry presents itself as the triumph of science. Yet its structure mirrors ancient pharmakeia:

- Alchemy to Chemistry: Medieval alchemists sought elixirs of life; modern chemists synthesize drugs of control.

- Patent Monopolies: Healing commodified, access restricted, profit prioritized.
- Symptom Management: Chronic conditions treated, but rarely cured... ensuring lifelong dependency.
- Psychopharmacology: Drugs altering mood, perception, and behavior... chemical enchantments for the modern age.

Pharmaceuticals are not all inherently evil. But the system built around them reflects pharmakeia: manipulation, dependency, and deception.

The Spell of Dependency

Pharmakeia binds populations through:
- Polypharmacy: Multiple prescriptions, often interacting, creating cycles of side effects and new prescriptions.
- Addiction: Opioids, benzodiazepines, and stimulants creating chemical bondage.
- Normalization: Children medicated for behavior, adults for mood, elders for longevity... life itself medicalized.
- Trust in Sorcerers: Doctors and corporations elevated as high priests of health, their decrees unquestioned.

This is not healing, it is enchantment. It is the spell of pharmakeia: dependency disguised as medicine.

The Symbols of Medicine: Serpents and Sorcery

The emblems of medicine reveal its spiritual undercurrent:

- Rod of Asclepius: A single serpent entwined around a staff, symbol of the Greek god Asclepius, son of Apollo, associated with healing temples and serpent cults.
- Caduceus: Two serpents entwined around a winged staff, carried by Hermes (Mercury), god of commerce, trickery, and boundaries.
- Modern Confusion: In the U.S., the caduceus is often used as a medical symbol, though historically it represents commerce and deception, not healing.

The serpent is central. In Eden, the serpent deceived. In Greek cults, the serpent healed. In modern medicine, the serpent remains the emblem. This is not a coincidence, it is continuity. The serpent is the symbol of pharmakeia: healing entwined with deception, medicine entwined with sorcery.

Pharmakeia and the Watchers' Plan

The Watchers once corrupted flesh through forbidden knowledge. Pharmakeia continues this project:

- Corruption of Flesh: Drugs altering biology, hormones, and reproduction.
- Clouding of Mind: Psychopharmacology dulling discernment, altering perception.
- Shortening of Days: Side effects, dependency, and chronic illness reducing vitality.
- Counterfeit Covenant: Trust in sorcerers replacing trust in GOD.

Pharmakeia is not merely medicine, it is manipulation. It is the Watchers' spell, binding humanity to a counterfeit table.

Pharmakeia and the Beast System

The Bible book of Revelation describes a Beast system where all nations are deceived by sorcery.

Pharmakeia is central to this system:

- Global Reach: Pharmaceuticals produced and distributed worldwide.
- Economic Power: Corporations wielding influence over governments and populations.
- Control of Flesh: Populations dependent on prescriptions for survival.
- Deception of Nations: Healing promised, but estrangement delivered.

Pharmakeia is not peripheral to the Watchers' plans, it is central to them. It is the spell by which nations are deceived, populations controlled, and covenant with GOD is further severed.

Resistance and Remembrance

To resist pharmakeia is not to reject all medicine, but to discern:

- Discernment: Recognizing when medicine heals and when it manipulates.
- Remembrance: Anchoring health in covenant with GOD, not sorcerers' spells.
- Accountability: Exposing abuses, monopolies, and deceptions.
- Covenant: Trusting in divine provision, not counterfeit enchantments.

The serpent may entwine the staff, but it does not hold the covenant. True healing comes not from pharmakeia, but from the hand of GOD.

Chapter 22 –
The Last Remembrance

"The eternal law is that light shall return."
— Zoroastrian hymn

The serpent's tactic is erasure; GOD's antidote is remembrance. Scripture, oral tradition, archaeology... all can help preserve memory. Hidden forces of preservation endure: angels, prophets, faithful communities. The story ends not with despair but with hope. The light shines in darkness, and the darkness cannot overcome it.

Their goal is to get humanity further from GOD

The serpent's tactic has always been erasure. From Eden to Babel, from the Watchers to the Beast system, the strategy is the same: sever memory, obscure covenant, and confuse identity. If humanity forgets who it is, it forgets whose it is.

If remembrance is lost, estrangement is complete.

But GOD's antidote is remembrance. Scripture, oral tradition, archaeology, and faithful testimony help preserve memory against erasure. Angels guard archives, prophets speak truth, and communities of faith carry remembrance across generations. The serpent whispers, "Forget." GOD commands, "REMEMBER."

This is the last remembrance: the final act of resistance against erasure. It is not despair but hope. For though the serpent seeks to erase, the light shines in darkness, and the darkness cannot overcome it. This war is real, but it is not endless. The good will prevail. GOD has not forsaken HIS people. The last remembrance is the assurance that covenant endures, memory survives, and victory is certain.

The Serpent's Tactic: Erasure

Throughout history, the serpent's strategy has been consistent:

- Erasure of Scripture: Suppression, distortion, or destruction of sacred texts.
- Erasure of Memory: Collective amnesia through confusion, deception, and manipulation.
- Erasure of Identity: Redefining humanity, severing it from the image of GOD.

- Erasure of Covenant: Replacing divine remembrance with counterfeit systems of control.

From the Watchers' corruption of flesh to the digital cage of surveillance, the serpent's goal is the same: erase remembrance, and covenant collapses.

GOD's Antidote: Remembrance

Against erasure, GOD commands remembrance:

- Scripture: The written Word preserved across millennia, copied, translated, and transmitted despite persecution.
- Oral Tradition: Stories carried by prophets, elders, and faithful communities, ensuring continuity even when texts were lost.
- Archaeology: Stones, inscriptions, and artifacts testifying to histories the serpent sought to erase.
- Sacraments and Rituals: Passover, communion, baptism... embodied acts of remembrance.

Remembrance is not passive, it is active resistance. To remember is to defy erasure. To remember is to remain in covenant with GOD.

Hidden Forces of Preservation

GOD has not left humanity defenseless. Hidden forces preserve memory:

- Angels: Guardians of archives, messengers of remembrance, protectors of covenantal truth.

- Prophets: Voices crying in the wilderness, calling people back to remembrance.
- Faithful Communities: Families, churches, and fellowships preserving testimony across generations.
- Martyrs: Witnesses whose blood became seed, ensuring remembrance through sacrifice.

These forces endure. They are the unseen custodians of memory, ensuring that the serpent's erasure is never complete.

The War of Memory

The war is not only over land or flesh, it is over memory:

- Digital Erasure: Archives deleted, histories rewritten, testimonies censored.
- Pharmakeia: Minds clouded, discernment dulled, remembrance severed.
- Financial Net: Access to commerce contingent on compliance, memory of covenant replaced by dependency.
- Ambiguity Strategy: Confusion sown, certainty eroded, remembrance destabilized.

Yet the war is not lost. For every act of erasure, there is an act of remembrance. For every whisper of the serpent, there is the WORD of GOD.

The Light in the Darkness

In the Bibles New Testament, John's Gospel declares: "The light shines in the darkness, and the darkness cannot overcome it."

This is the last remembrance: that no matter how deep the erasure, no matter how strong the deception, the light endures.

- Hope in Scripture: The Word preserved, unbroken, unchanging.
- Hope in Testimony: Witnesses across generations, refusing to forget.
- Hope in Victory: The assurance that the war ends not in defeat, but in triumph.

The serpent's tactic is erasure. GOD's antidote is remembrance. And remembrance will prevail.

The Assurance of Victory

This is not a war of equals. The serpent is cunning, but GOD is sovereign. The Watchers may corrupt, but angels preserve. The Beast may deceive, but GOD conquers.

- GOD Has Not Forsaken Us: His Spirit brings remembrance (John 14:26).
- The Good Will Win: The war ends with victory, not defeat.
- Remembrance Endures: Memory cannot be erased, for GOD Himself remembers His covenant.
- Hope Is Certain: The last remembrance is not despair... it is triumph.

OUR story ends not with darkness, but with LIGHT. Not with erasure, but with REMEMBRANCE. Not with defeat, but with VICTORY. HIS VICTORY.

Conclusion –
The Call to Remembrance

The strategy of the Watchers and the serpents has always been erasure. From Eden's whisper from one of the serpents to the Watchers' corruption, from pharmakeia's spell to the digital cage, the tactic is the same: confuse, distort, and sever remembrance. If humanity forgets its covenant, it forgets its CREATOR. If memory is erased, identity collapses.

But GOD's antidote is remembrance. Scripture, testimony, archaeology, and faithful communities and individuals preserve memory against erasure. Angels guard archives. Prophets cry out. Families pass down stories. GOD HIMSELF brings remembrance to the heart.

This book has traced the evil strategies of the Watchers across flesh, food, finance, and memory. It has shown how the Watchers' forbidden knowledge echoes in modern systems of control. Yet the story does not end in despair. It ends in hope. For light shines in darkness, and the darkness cannot overcome it.

The Threads Pulled Together

- Flesh: Corrupted by hybridization, pharmakeia, and genetic manipulation... yet redeemed in man and the son of man, the true Image of GOD.
- Food: Altered by additives and pesticides... yet covenant meals like Passover preserve remembrance.

- Finance: Centralized into nets of control... yet GOD provides daily bread and commands trust, not servitude.
- Memory: Attacked by ambiguity, Mandela Effects, and digital erasure... yet preserved in Scripture, testimony, and Spirit.

Every tactic of estrangement has its antidote in remembrance. Every counterfeit has its true covenantal counterpart.

The Hidden Custodians of Hope

Even in the darkest times, GOD preserves a remnant:
- Angels: Guardians of archives and messengers of truth.
- Prophets: Voices calling people back to covenant.
- Communities of Faith: Families, churches, and fellowships carrying memory across generations.
- Martyrs and Witnesses: Lives laid down so remembrance would not die.

They cannot erase what GOD preserves. They cannot sever what GOD sustains.

The War Already Won

This is not a war of equals. The Watchers and the serpents are cunning, but GOD is sovereign. The Beast may rise, but GOD conquers. The famine of truth may spread, but the Bread of Life endures.

- GOD Has Not Forsaken Us: HIS Spirit brings remembrance.
- Victory Is Assured: The war ends not in defeat, but in triumph.

- Remembrance Endures: GOD remembers HIS covenant forever.
- Hope Is Certain: The last remembrance is not despair... it is triumph.

Their tactic is erasure. GOD's antidote is remembrance. And remembrance will prevail.

A Call to the Reader

This is not only history... it is invitation. You, the reader, are part of the last remembrance. Every prayer, every testimony, every act of faith is resistance against erasure. Every meal shared in covenant, every Scripture recited, every truth preserved is a blow against the strategy of the Watchers and the serpents.

You are not forsaken. You are not powerless. You are part of the remnant, the community of remembrance, the people of covenant. The war is real, but the victory is certain. The light shines in darkness, and the darkness cannot overcome it.

Remember. Resist. Endure. Hope.

Appendix – Master Bibliography of Sources

This consolidated bibliography gathers all verifiable references cited across Chapters 1–22. It is organized by Chapter for clarity.

Appendix – Chapter 1 Sources

Scriptural References
- Genesis 3:1–6 — The serpent's temptation and the fall
- Genesis 4:1–16 — Cain and Abel, the first murder
- 1 Enoch 6–8 — The descent of the Watchers and forbidden knowledge
- Revelation 12:9 — The serpent as Satan, the deceiver of the whole world

Comparative Mythology
- Epic of Gilgamesh, Tablet XI — Serpent stealing the plant of life
- Egyptian Book of the Dead — Uraeus serpent symbolism
- Mesoamerican Codices — Quetzalcoatl as feathered serpent
- Hindu Puranas — Naga beings and subterranean realms
- Norse Eddas — Jörmungandr, the world serpent

Secondary Scholarship
- Michael Heiser, The Unseen Realm — Divine council and serpent motifs
- Mircea Eliade, Patterns in Comparative Religion — Serpent symbolism across cultures
- Annette Yoshiko Reed, Fallen Angels and the History of Judaism and Christianity — Cain traditions and Watcher lore
- Karel van der Toorn, Scribal Culture and the Making of the Hebrew Bible — Kenite scribes and textual transmission

Online Resources
- Sefaria.org — Hebrew texts and commentaries
- EarlyJewishWritings.com — Apocryphal and pseudepigraphal sources

• BibleGateway.com — Scriptural translations and cross-references

Appendix – Chapter 2 Sources

Scriptural References
• Genesis 6:1–13 — Corruption of flesh and divine judgment
• Genesis 7–9 — The Flood narrative and Noah's preservation
• 1 Enoch 6–16 — The descent of the Watchers and the origin of the Nephilim
• 2 Peter 2:4 — Angels bound in chains of darkness
• Jude 1:6 — Angels who left their proper domain
• Genesis 10:15–18 — Post-Flood descendants of Canaan, including giants

Comparative Mythology
• Epic of Gilgamesh, Tablet XI — Flood narrative and divine reset
• Sumerian King List — Pre-Flood kings and their long reigns
• Zoroastrian texts — Cataclysmic floods and preservation of righteous seed
• Hopi oral tradition — Destruction of previous worlds by water

Secondary Scholarship
• Michael Heiser, Reversing Hermon — Watchers, Nephilim, and New Testament echoes
• Annette Yoshiko Reed, Fallen Angels and the History of Judaism and Christianity — Enochic traditions and post-Flood demonology
• Gordon Wenham, Word Biblical Commentary: Genesis 1–15 — Exegetical insights on Genesis 6
• John Walton, The Lost World of Genesis One — Ancient Near Eastern context of creation and flood

Online Resources
- Sefaria.org — Hebrew texts and commentaries on Genesis and Enoch
- EarlyJewishWritings.com — Full text of 1 Enoch and related pseudepigrapha
- BibleGateway.com — Scriptural translations and cross-references
- USGS Flood Archives — Geological evidence of ancient flood events

Appendix – Chapter 3 Sources

Scriptural References
- Genesis 4:22 — Tubal-Cain as instructor in metallurgy
- Genesis 15:19 — The Kenites listed among the peoples of Canaan
- Numbers 24:21–22 — Balaam's oracle concerning the Kenites
- Judges 1:16 — The Kenites traveling with Judah
- 1 Samuel 15:6 — Saul sparing the Kenites during Amalek's destruction
- Exodus 18 — Jethro (a Kenite priest) advising Moses

Comparative Mythology & Tradition
- 1 Enoch 6–8 — Watchers teaching metallurgy, enchantments, and writing
- Jubilees 4 — Cain's descendants and the origins of crafts
- Ancient Near Eastern texts on smith-gods (e.g., Kothar-wa-Hasis in Ugaritic myth)
- Greek myth of Hephaestus — divine smith and craftsman

Secondary Scholarship

- Michael Heiser, The Unseen Realm — Divine council worldview and Cainite traditions
- Karel van der Toorn, Scribal Culture and the Making of the Hebrew Bible — The role of scribes in preserving and shaping tradition
- Mircea Eliade, The Forge and the Crucible — Metallurgy as sacred and transformative knowledge
- John Day, In Search of Pre-Exilic Israel — Kenites and Midianites in Israel's early history

Online Resources
- Sefaria.org — Hebrew texts and rabbinic commentary on Cain and the Kenites
- EarlyJewishWritings.com — Jubilees and Enochic traditions
- BibleGateway.com — Scriptural translations and cross-references
- University of Chicago Oriental Institute — Studies on metallurgy in the ancient Near East

Appendix – Chapter 4 Sources

Scriptural References
- Genesis 6:1–4 — Sons of GOD and daughters of men
- Leviticus 16:8–10 — The scapegoat "for Azazel"
- 2 Peter 2:4 — Angels bound in chains of darkness
- Jude 1:6 — Angels who left their proper domain

Apocryphal & Pseudepigraphal Texts
- 1 Enoch 6–16 — The descent of the Watchers, their oath, their teachings, and their judgment
- Jubilees 5 — The corruption of flesh and the binding of the Watchers

- Dead Sea Scrolls (4Q201–4Q204) — Fragments of the Book of Giants

Comparative Mythology
- Mesopotamian Apkallu — semi-divine sages who taught forbidden arts before the Flood
- Greek myths of the Titans — divine beings bound in Tartarus after rebellion
- Zoroastrian daevas — fallen spirits who corrupt creation

Secondary Scholarship
- Michael Heiser, Reversing Hermon — The Watchers' role in New Testament theology
- Annette Yoshiko Reed, Fallen Angels and the History of Judaism and Christianity — Development of Enochic traditions
- Loren Stuckenbruck, The Book of Giants from Qumran — Analysis of Nephilim traditions
- Mircea Eliade, Patterns in Comparative Religion — Cross-cultural serpent and giant motifs

Online Resources
- Sefaria.org — Hebrew texts and commentary on Leviticus and Enoch
- EarlyJewishWritings.com — Full text of 1 Enoch and Jubilees
- Dead Sea Scrolls Digital Library — Fragments of the Book of Giants
- BibleGateway.com — Scriptural translations and cross-references

Appendix – Chapter 5 Sources

Scriptural References
- Genesis 6:1–4 — The sons of GOD and the daughters of men

- 1 Enoch 6–10 — The descent of the two hundred angels and their oath
- Revelation 8:10–11 — A great star falling from heaven
- Revelation 12:7–9 — The war in heaven and the casting down of angels

Geological & Archaeological Sources
- USGS Earth Impact Database — Catalog of confirmed impact craters
- NASA Earth Observatory — Satellite imagery of impact structures
- Barringer Crater (Arizona, USA) — Geological surveys and preservation studies
- Chicxulub Crater (Mexico) — Alvarez hypothesis and extinction event research
- Vredefort Dome (South Africa) — UNESCO World Heritage documentation
- Sudbury Basin (Canada) — Geological and mining studies
- Lonar Crater (India) — UNESCO and Indian Geological Survey reports
- Manicouagan Crater (Canada) — Remote sensing and hydrological studies
- Popigai Crater (Russia) — Russian Academy of Sciences research
- Wolfe Creek Crater (Australia) — Aboriginal traditions and geological surveys

Comparative Mythology
- Aboriginal Dreamtime stories of Wolfe Creek Crater
- Hindu traditions of Lonar Crater as a site of divine wrath
- Mesoamerican myths of fire from the sky (linked to Chicxulub region)
- Norse Eddas — Stars falling at Ragnarök

- Sibylline Oracles — Stars falling as judgment

Secondary Scholarship
- Immanuel Velikovsky, Worlds in Collision — Catastrophism and cosmic intrusion
- David Keys, Catastrophe — Global disasters and cultural resets
- Mircea Eliade, The Myth of the Eternal Return — Cyclical destruction and renewal
- Adrian Tinniswood, By Permission of Heaven — Fires as resets in London
- Ross Miller, American Apocalypse — The Great Fire of Chicago

Online Resources
- Earth Impact Database (University of New Brunswick)
- NASA Earth Observatory archives
- Tunguska Event archives (Russian Academy of Sciences)
- National Archives (London, Chicago, San Francisco fire records)

Appendix – Chapter 6 Sources

Scriptural References
- Psalm 64:6 — Hidden counsels in the depths of the heart
- Isaiah 29:15 — Those who hide their counsel in the dark
- Ezekiel 8:7–12 — Secret chambers beneath the Temple
- Psalm 82 — GOD judging among the divine council
- 2 Peter 2:4 — Angels bound in chains of darkness

Comparative Mythology
- Hopi oral traditions — The Ant People and subterranean refuge
- Greek mythology — Hades and the underworld councils

- Norse mythology — Svartálfaheimr, the subterranean realm of dwarves
- Hindu Puranas — Nagas and the kingdom of Pātāla
- Tibetan & Central Asian lore — Shambhala and Agartha traditions

Archaeology & History
- Derinkuyu Underground City (Turkey) — UNESCO World Heritage documentation
- Hypogeum of Ħal-Saflieni (Malta) — Archaeological studies of subterranean temples
- Chavín de Huántar (Peru) — Ritual galleries and labyrinths
- Ellora and Ajanta Caves (India) — Rock-cut subterranean temples
- Naours Tunnels (France) — Rediscovered subterranean city

Secondary Scholarship
- Mircea Eliade, The Forge and the Crucible — Subterranean symbolism in metallurgy and ritual
- Michael Heiser, The Unseen Realm — Divine council worldview
- Graham Hancock, Underworld — Submerged and subterranean civilizations
- Karel van der Toorn, Scribal Culture and the Making of the Hebrew Bible — Hidden archives and scribal traditions

Online Resources
- UNESCO World Heritage Centre — Documentation of subterranean sites
- Sefaria.org — Hebrew texts and commentaries on Ezekiel and Psalms
- EarlyJewishWritings.com — Apocryphal traditions of Tartarus and the Watchers

- Archaeology.org — Features on Derinkuyu, Hypogeum, and subterranean complexes

Appendix – Chapter 7 Sources

Scriptural References
- Psalm 82 — GOD presiding in the divine council
- Isaiah 29:15 — Hidden counsels in the dark
- Ezekiel 8:7–12 — Secret chambers beneath the Temple
- 1 Enoch 10–15 — Watchers bound in subterranean prisons
- Jubilees 5 — Angels confined until judgment
- Revelation 9 — The abyss opened, releasing beings

Comparative Mythology
- Hopi oral traditions — The Ant People and subterranean refuge
- Greek mythology — Hades and the underworld councils
- Norse mythology — Hel and her court
- Hindu Puranas — Nagas and the kingdom of Pātāla
- Tibetan & Central Asian lore — Shambhala and Agartha

Archaeology & History
- Derinkuyu Underground City (Turkey) — Archaeological surveys
- Hypogeum of Hal-Saflieni (Malta) — UNESCO documentation
- Chavín de Huántar (Peru) — Ritual galleries and subterranean labyrinths
- Ellora and Ajanta Caves (India) — Rock-cut subterranean temples
- Naours Tunnels (France) — Rediscovered subterranean city

Secondary Scholarship

- Michael Heiser, The Unseen Realm — Divine council worldview
- Mircea Eliade, The Forge and the Crucible — Subterranean symbolism
- Graham Hancock, Underworld — Submerged and subterranean civilizations
- Annette Yoshiko Reed, Fallen Angels and the History of Judaism and Christianity — Watcher traditions
- Karel van der Toorn, Scribal Culture and the Making of the Hebrew Bible — Hidden archives

Online Resources
- UNESCO World Heritage Centre — Documentation of subterranean sites
- Sefaria.org — Hebrew texts and commentaries
- EarlyJewishWritings.com — Apocryphal traditions of Tartarus and the Watchers
- Archaeology.org — Features on Derinkuyu, Hypogeum, and subterranean complexes

Appendix – Chapter 8 Sources

Scriptural References
- Genesis 4:22 — Tubal-Cain as instructor in metallurgy
- Genesis 15:19 — The Kenites listed among the peoples of Canaan
- Exodus 18 — Jethro advising Moses
- Judges 1:16 — The Kenites traveling with Judah
- 1 Samuel 15:6 — Saul sparing the Kenites
- Numbers 24:21–22 — Balaam's prophecy concerning the Kenites

Comparative Mythology & Tradition

- 1 Enoch 6–8 — Watchers teaching metallurgy and enchantments
- Jubilees 4 — Cain's descendants and the origins of crafts
- Ancient Near Eastern texts on smith-gods (e.g., Kothar-wa-Hasis in Ugaritic myth)
- Greek myth of Hephaestus — divine smith and craftsman

Archaeology & History
- Excavations in Timna Valley (Israel) — Ancient copper mining and metallurgy
- Ugaritic texts — Smith-gods and scribal traditions
- Egyptian records — Scribes as custodians of memory

Secondary Scholarship
- Michael Heiser, The Unseen Realm — Divine council worldview and Cainite traditions
- Karel van der Toorn, Scribal Culture and the Making of the Hebrew Bible — The role of scribes in shaping tradition
- Mircea Eliade, The Forge and the Crucible — Metallurgy as sacred knowledge
- John Day, In Search of Pre-Exilic Israel — Kenites and Midianites in Israel's early history

Online Resources
- Sefaria.org — Hebrew texts and rabbinic commentary on Cain and the Kenites
- EarlyJewishWritings.com — Jubilees and Enochic traditions
- BibleGateway.com — Scriptural translations and cross-references
- Archaeology.org — Features on Timna Valley metallurgy

Appendix – Chapter 9 Sources

Scriptural References

- Genesis 6–9 — The Flood of Noah
- Genesis 19 — Fire on Sodom and Gomorrah
- Exodus 19 — Sinai in fire
- 2 Kings 1:10–12 — Fire from heaven consuming captains
- 2 Peter 3:5–7 — The world destroyed by water, reserved for fire
- Revelation 8:7–11 — Fire and falling stars as judgment

Comparative Mythology

- Epic of Gilgamesh, Tablet XI — Flood narrative
- Sumerian King List — Kingship before and after the flood
- Hopi oral traditions — Ant People and subterranean refuge
- Hindu Puranas — Cycles of fire and flood
- Norse Eddas — Ragnarök and fiery destruction
- Zoroastrian texts — Purification by molten metal

Archaeology & History

- Pompeii (Italy) — Preservation in volcanic ash
- Library of Alexandria — Accounts of destruction by fire
- Nile Floods (Egypt) — Annual cycles of destruction and renewal
- Yellow River Floods (China) — Historical and mythic accounts
- Great Fire of London (1666) — Urban erasure and rebirth
- Great Fire of Chicago (1871) — Mythic meaning of destruction
- San Francisco Earthquake and Fire (1906) — Erasure of archives

Secondary Scholarship

- David Keys, Catastrophe — Global disasters and cultural resets
- Mircea Eliade, The Myth of the Eternal Return — Cyclical destruction and renewal

- Adrian Tinniswood, By Permission of Heaven — The Great Fire of London
- Ross Miller, American Apocalypse — The Great Fire of Chicago
- Philip Fradkin, The Great Earthquake and Firestorms of 1906

Online Resources
- Sefaria.org — Hebrew texts and commentaries
- EarlyJewishWritings.com — Apocryphal flood and fire traditions
- BibleGateway.com — Scriptural translations and cross-references
- Archaeology.org — Features on Pompeii, Alexandria, and flood archaeology

Appendix – Chapter 10 Sources

Scriptural References
- Genesis 6–9 — The Flood as erasure and preservation
- Genesis 19 — Fire on Sodom and Gomorrah
- 2 Peter 3:5–7 — The world destroyed by water, reserved for fire
- Revelation 6:4 — The red horse of war, taking peace from the earth
- Revelation 8:7 — Fire and blood cast upon the earth

Historical Sources
- John Keegan, The First World War — Comprehensive history of WWI
- Antony Beevor, The Second World War — Global history of WWII
- Richard Overy, The Bombing War — Civilian destruction in WWII

- Raul Hilberg, The Destruction of the European Jews — Holocaust as erasure
- Margaret MacMillan, The War That Ended Peace — Causes of WWI

Comparative Mythology
- Heraclitus — "War is the father of all things"
- Hindu Puranas — Cycles of destruction and renewal
- Norse Eddas — Ragnarök as fiery destruction and rebirth
- Zoroastrian texts — Purification by fire

Archaeology & Memory
- Commonwealth War Graves Commission — Memorialization of WWI dead
- Yad Vashem (Jerusalem) — Holocaust remembrance
- Hiroshima Peace Memorial — Preservation of atomic memory
- National Archives (UK, US, Germany, Russia) — Records of war and destruction

Secondary Scholarship
- David Keys, Catastrophe — Disasters as cultural resets
- Mircea Eliade, The Myth of the Eternal Return — Cyclical destruction and renewal
- Jay Winter, Sites of Memory, Sites of Mourning — Remembrance after WWI
- Modris Eksteins, Rites of Spring — Cultural transformation through WWI

Online Resources
- Imperial War Museums (UK) — WWI and WWII archives
- United States Holocaust Memorial Museum — Holocaust documentation
- UNESCO World Heritage — Hiroshima Peace Memorial

• National WWII Museum (New Orleans) — Global WWII history

Appendix – Chapter 11 Sources

Scriptural References
• Genesis 6:4 — Giants before and after the Flood
• Deuteronomy 2–3 — Rephaim, Anakim, and giant clans
• 1 Samuel 17 — Goliath of Gath
• Mark 5:1–20 — Legion and the Gerasene demoniac
• Matthew 12:43–45 — Wandering unclean spirits
• Revelation 9 — Spirits released from the abyss

Apocryphal & Pseudepigraphal Texts
• 1 Enoch 15–16 — Evil spirits of the giants
• Jubilees 10 — Binding of Nephilim spirits
• Dead Sea Scrolls (Book of Giants) — Dreams and fears of the giants
• Midrashic traditions — Og and Nephilim survival

Comparative Mythology
• Mesopotamian Pazuzu — Wind demon
• Greek Titans and Gigantes — Spirits in Tartarus
• Norse Draugr — Undead warriors
• Hindu Asuras — Spirits of rebellion
• Mesoamerican Tzitzimime — Star demons

Archaeology & History
• Excavations at Bashan — Sites linked to Og and Rephaim
• Ugaritic texts — Spirits and underworld beings
• Temple architecture — Designs to repel or contain spirits

Secondary Scholarship
• Michael Heiser, Reversing Hermon — Nephilim and New Testament theology
• Annette Yoshiko Reed, Fallen Angels and the History of Judaism and Christianity — Development of Nephilim traditions
• Loren Stuckenbruck, The Myth of Rebellious Angels — Enochic demonology
• Mircea Eliade, various books

Appendix – Chapter 12 Sources

Scriptural References
• Genesis 6:4 — Giants before and after the Flood
• 1 Enoch 15:8–12 — Spirits of the giants becoming evil spirits (demons)
• Jubilees 10 — Binding of Nephilim spirits, leaving some to test humanity
• Matthew 12:43–45 — Unclean spirits wandering, seeking rest
• Revelation 9 — Beings released from the abyss
• 2 Thessalonians 2:9–11 — Strong delusion sent upon those who believe lies

Apocryphal & Pseudepigraphal Texts
• Book of Giants (Dead Sea Scrolls) — Dreams and fears of the Nephilim
• Testament of Solomon — Demons and their functions
• Zohar — Esoteric traditions of hybrid beings and spiritual corruption

Comparative Mythology

- Mesopotamian Apkallu — Semi-divine sages with forbidden knowledge
- Greek Gigantes — Defeated giants whose spirits linger in Tartarus
- Norse Draugr — Restless undead haunting the living
- Hindu Asuras — Beings of rebellion and deception
- Mesoamerican Tzitzimime — Star demons descending to devour humanity

Modern Folklore & Ufology
- Whitley Strieber, Communion — Abduction narratives involving Greys
- John Mack, Abduction — Psychological and spiritual dimensions
- Jacques Vallée, Passport to Magonia — Folklore continuity in UFO encounters
- David Jacobs, The Threat — Hybridization programs and control
- Linda Moulton Howe, Glimpses of Other Realities — Biological engineering and Greys

Secondary Scholarship
- Michael Heiser, Reversing Hermon — Watchers, Nephilim, and New Testament theology
- Annette Yoshiko Reed, Fallen Angels and the History of Judaism and Christianity

Appendix – Chapter 13 Sources

Scriptural References
- Genesis 6:1–4 — Sons of GOD, daughters of men, and the Nephilim

- 1 Enoch 6–16 — Watchers, forbidden knowledge, and hybrid offspring
- Jubilees 5, 10 — Binding of spirits and continuation of corruption
- Isaiah 29:15 — Those who hide their counsel in the deep
- Revelation 9 — Beings released from the abyss

Apocryphal & Pseudepigraphal Texts
- Book of Giants (Dead Sea Scrolls) — Dreams and fears of the Nephilim
- Testament of Solomon — Demons and their functions
- Zohar — Esoteric traditions of hybrid beings

Comparative Mythology
- Hopi Ant People — Subterranean beings preserving humanity
- Greek Hades — Custodians of the underworld
- Norse Dwarves — Subterranean smiths and guardians
- Hindu Nagas — Serpent-kings in Pātāla
- Tibetan Shambhala — Hidden subterranean rulers

Archaeology & History
- Derinkuyu and Kaymakli (Cappadocia, Turkey) — Vast underground cities
- Mount Shasta (California, USA) — Legends of hidden cities and portals
- Dulce Base (New Mexico, USA) — Alleged joint human-Grey facility
- Hypogeum of Hal-Saflieni (Malta) — Subterranean temple complex

Modern Folklore & Ufology
- Whitley Strieber, Communion — Abduction narratives

- John Mack, Abduction — Psychological and spiritual dimensions
- Jacques Vallée, Passport to Magonia — Folklore continuity in UFO encounters
- David Jacobs, The Threat — Hybridization programs
- Linda Moulton Howe, Glimpses of Other Realities — Underground bases and Greys

Secondary Scholarship
- Michael Heiser, Reversing Hermon — Watchers and genetic corruption
- Annette Yoshiko Reed, Fallen Angels and the History of Judaism and Christianity
- Mircea Eliade, The Forge and the Crucible — Subterranean symbolism
- Graham Hancock, Underworld — Submerged and subterranean civilizations

Online Resources
- Sefaria.org — Hebrew texts and commentaries
- EarlyJewishWritings.com — Apocryphal and pseudepigraphal texts
- BibleGateway.com

Appendix – Chapter 14 Sources

Scriptural References
- Genesis 3:1–5 — The serpent's ambiguous question
- Genesis 6:1–4 — The Nephilim and corruption of flesh
- 1 Enoch 6–16 — Watchers' partial revelations
- Isaiah 29:15 — Hidden counsels in the dark
- Matthew 24:37 — "As in the days of Noah…"
- 2 Thessalonians 2:9–11 — Strong delusion and deception

Apocryphal & Pseudepigraphal Texts
- Book of Giants — Fragmentary testimonies of Nephilim corruption
- Jubilees 5, 10 — Binding of spirits, continuation of corruption
- Testament of Solomon — Demons and their deceptive strategies

Comparative Mythology
- Greek Oracles — Ambiguous prophecies, destabilizing kings
- Norse Loki — Trickster figure sowing doubt and division
- Hindu Maya — Illusion and ambiguity as cosmic deception
- Mesoamerican Tezcatlipoca — God of smoke and mirrors, confusion and corruption

Modern Folklore & Ufology
- Whitley Strieber, Communion — Ambiguous abduction memories
- John Mack, Abduction — Psychological ambiguity of encounters
- Jacques Vallée, Passport to Magonia — Folklore continuity in UFO ambiguity
- David Jacobs, The Threat — Hybridization and elusive evidence
- Linda Moulton Howe, Glimpses of Other Realities — Ambiguous testimonies and contradictions

Secondary Scholarship
- Michael Heiser, Reversing Hermon — Watchers and partial revelations
- Annette Yoshiko Reed, Fallen Angels and the History of Judaism and Christianity

- Mircea Eliade, Myth and Reality — Ambiguity in mythic structures
- Carl Jung, Flying Saucers: A Modern Myth of Things Seen in the Skies — UFOs as psychological ambiguity

Online Resources
- Sefaria.org — Hebrew texts and commentaries
- EarlyJewishWritings.com — Apocryphal and pseudepigraphal texts
- BibleGateway.com — Scriptural translations and cross-references
- National UFO Reporting Center — Catalog of ambiguous sightings

Appendix – Chapter 15 Sources

Scriptural References
- Genesis 6:1–4 — Corruption of flesh and manipulation of creation
- 1 Enoch 6–8 — Watchers teaching forbidden astronomy and manipulation of the heavens
- Isaiah 29:15 — Those who hide their counsel in the deep
- Luke 21:26 — Powers of the heavens shaken
- Psalm 19:1 — The heavens declare the glory of GOD

Historical Precedents
- Operation Sea-Spray (1950, San Francisco) — U.S. Navy biological dispersal
- Operation LAC (1957–58, Midwest USA) — U.S. Army aerosol dispersal
- UK Ministry of Defence dispersals (1940s–1970s) — Biological and chemical releases over populations

Geoengineering and Weather Modification
- U.S. National Academy of Sciences (2015) — Reports on geoengineering
- Harvard Solar Geoengineering Research Program — Stratospheric aerosol injection studies
- UK Royal Society (2009) — Report on climate intervention
- UN Convention on the Prohibition of Military or Any Other Hostile Use of Environmental Modification Techniques (ENMOD, 1978)

Comparative Mythology
- Mesopotamian Watchers — Manipulation of the heavens
- Greek Uranus — The sky as a realm of control and conflict
- Norse Ymir — The sky formed from a slain giant, manipulated by gods
- Hindu Indra — Weather manipulation as divine weapon

Secondary Scholarship
- Clive Hamilton, Earthmasters: The Dawn of the Age of Climate Engineering
- Alan Robock, Benefits and Risks of Stratospheric Geoengineering
- Michael Heiser, The Unseen Realm — Watchers and manipulation of the firmament
- Mircea Eliade, Patterns in Comparative Religion — Sky as sacred and corrupted

Online Resources
- NASA and NOAA reports on contrails and geoengineering
- Declassified U.S. Army and UK MoD documents on dispersal tests
- IPCC reports on climate intervention risks
- Archive.org — Preservation of whistleblower testimonies

Appendix – Chapter 16 Sources

Scriptural References
- Genesis 1:27 — Humanity created in GOD's image
- Genesis 3:5 — "Ye shall be as gods"
- Genesis 6:1–4 — Corruption of flesh by the Watchers
- 1 Enoch 6–16 — Forbidden knowledge and hybridization
- Revelation 13 — The Beast system and the mark
- 2 Thessalonians 2:9–11 — Strong delusion

Historical Abuses
- Tuskegee Syphilis Study (1932–1972) — U.S. Public Health Service
- Guatemala Experiments (1946–1948) — U.S. government medical testing
- MK-ULTRA (1950s–1970s) — CIA mind control program
- Operation Sea-Spray (1950) — U.S. Navy biological dispersal

Biotechnology and mRNA
- National Institutes of Health — mRNA vaccine research
- Moderna and Pfizer publications on mRNA platforms
- World Health Organization reports on genetic technologies
- Scholarly articles on CRISPR and gene editing

Comparative Mythology
- Mesopotamian Apkallu — Semi-divine beings altering creation
- Greek Prometheus — Giver of fire, punished for transgression
- Norse Loki — Trickster altering forms and boundaries
- Hindu Asuras — Beings who sought immortality through forbidden means

Secondary Scholarship
- Michael Heiser, Reversing Hermon — Watchers and genetic corruption
- Annette Yoshiko Reed, Fallen Angels and the History of Judaism and Christianity
- Francis Fukuyama, Our Posthuman Future — Transhumanism and biotechnology
- Yuval Noah Harari, Homo Deus — Ambitions to transcend humanity
- Mircea Eliade, The Forge and the Crucible — Transformation and corruption of flesh

Online Resources
- CDC and NIH archives on vaccine history
- Declassified CIA documents on MK-ULTRA
- WHO reports on genetic engineering and bioethics
- Sefaria.org — Hebrew texts and commentaries
- BibleGateway.com — Scriptural translations and cross-references

Appendix – Chapter 17 Sources

Scriptural references
- Genesis 6:1–4 — Corruption of flesh and estrangement
- Psalm 104 — Creation's provision and the ecology of nourishment
- Daniel 1 — Dietary discernment and clarity
- Proverbs 23 — Appetite, deception, and discipline

Food systems and public health
- Michael Pollan — The Omnivore's Dilemma; In Defense of Food
- Marion Nestle — Food Politics; What to Eat

- Carlos Monteiro — NOVA classification of food processing and health impacts
- Robert Lustig — Metabolic effects of sugar and fructose
- Tim Spector — Microbiome and dietary diversity

Additives and packaging
- Research on emulsifiers and intestinal permeability
- Literature on artificial colors and child behavior
- Reviews on omega-6/omega-3 balance and inflammation
- Endocrine Society statements on EDCs (BPA, phthalates, PFAS)

Pesticides and residues
- Organophosphate exposure and neurodevelopment
- Glyphosate debates: carcinogenicity, microbiome, endocrine effects
- Neonicotinoids and ecological consequences
- Post-harvest treatments and consumer exposure

Comparative and ecological frames
- Vandana Shiva — Monocultures of the Mind
- Raj Patel — Stuffed and Starved
- David Montgomery — Dirt: The Erosion of Civilizations (soil health and nutrition)

Systems and policy
- Reports on food deserts, marketing to children, and structural nutrition inequities
- Analyses of ultra-processed food markets and chronic disease burden
- Discussions on precautionary principles in food additives and residues

Appendix – Chapter 18 Sources

Scriptural References
- Genesis 3:1 — The serpent's ambiguous question
- Genesis 6:1–4 — Corruption of flesh and estrangement
- Amos 8:11–12 — Famine of truth
- John 14:26 — The Spirit bringing remembrance
- Revelation 13 — The Beast system of deception

Psychological Explanations
- Elizabeth Loftus — Research on false memories and misinformation effect
- Frederic Bartlett — Schema theory of memory reconstruction
- Daniel Schacter — The Seven Sins of Memory

Quantum and Multiverse Hypotheses
- Hugh Everett — Many-Worlds Interpretation
- David Deutsch — Quantum computation and parallel realities
- Popular discussions linking CERN to reality anomalies

Technological Manipulation
- Declassified MK-ULTRA documents — Memory manipulation experiments
- Research on electromagnetic influence on cognition
- Studies on digital misinformation and archival tampering

Comparative Mythology
- Trickster archetypes: Loki (Norse), Coyote (Native American), Tezcatlipoca (Mesoamerican)
- The "Last Boktoon" as a parable of confusion and estrangement

Secondary Scholarship

- Michael Heiser, The Unseen Realm — Divine council and deception
- Mircea Eliade, Myth and Reality — Archetypes of confusion
- Jacques Vallée, Messengers of Deception — UFOs and manipulation of belief

Online Resources
- Mandela Effect community archives and case studies
- CERN public reports on particle collisions
- Psychology Today articles on false memory phenomena
- BibleGateway.com — Scriptural translations and cross-references

Appendix – Chapter 19 Sources

Scriptural References
- Genesis 6:1–4 — Corruption of flesh and estrangement
- Amos 8:11–12 — Famine of truth
- Revelation 13:16–17 — The mark of the Beast and control of commerce
- John 14:26 — The Spirit bringing remembrance
- Daniel 7:25 — The Beast seeking to change times and laws

Surveillance and Control
- Edward Snowden, Permanent Record — Revelations on PRISM and NSA surveillance
- Shoshana Zuboff, The Age of Surveillance Capitalism — Data as a tool of control
- Yuval Noah Harari, Homo Deus — Dataism and the future of humanity
- Reports on China's Social Credit System (2014–present)
- Studies on facial recognition and biometric surveillance

Artificial Intelligence
- Nick Bostrom, Superintelligence — AI as existential risk
- Kate Crawford, Atlas of AI — AI as extraction and control
- Research on algorithmic bias and predictive policing

Comparative Mythology
- Watchers (1 Enoch) — Corruption of flesh and forbidden knowledge
- Serpent in Eden — Ambiguity and manipulation
- Trickster archetypes — Control through deception

Secondary Scholarship
- Michael Heiser, The Unseen Realm — Divine council worldview
- Mircea Eliade, Myth and Reality — Archetypes of control and estrangement
- Jacques Ellul, The Technological Society — Technology as autonomous force

Online Resources
- PRISM program documents (2013 leaks)
- Reports on social credit systems (China, pilot programs elsewhere)
- NGO reports on digital rights and surveillance
- BibleGateway.com — Scriptural translations and cross-references

Appendix – Chapter 20 Sources

Scriptural References
- Proverbs 22:7 — The borrower is servant to the lender
- Amos 8:11–12 — Famine of truth

- Revelation 13:16–17 — The mark of the Beast and control of commerce
- Matthew 6:24 — Cannot serve GOD and mammon
- 1 Timothy 6:10 — The love of money as root of evil

Financial History
- Niall Ferguson, The Ascent of Money — History of finance and empires
- Liaquat Ahamed, Lords of Finance — Central banks and global crises
- Barry Eichengreen, Exorbitant Privilege — The dollar and global power

Surveillance and Control
- Edward Snowden, Permanent Record — Revelations on financial surveillance
- Shoshana Zuboff, The Age of Surveillance Capitalism — Data as control
- Reports on SWIFT sanctions and financial exclusion

Blockchain and Digital Currencies
- Satoshi Nakamoto, Bitcoin White Paper (2008)
- BIS (Bank for International Settlements) reports on CBDCs
- IMF and World Bank publications on digital finance
- Scholarly debates on blockchain transparency and surveillance

Comparative Mythology
- Watchers (1 Enoch) — The Table of corruption
- Ancient banquets as symbols of allegiance and control
- Trickster archetypes offering counterfeit gifts

Secondary Scholarship

- Michael Heiser, The Unseen Realm — Divine council worldview
- Jacques Ellul, The Technological Society — Technology as autonomous force
- Mircea Eliade, Myth and Reality — Archetypes of control and estrangement

Online Resources
- Central bank reports on CBDC pilots (China, EU, U.S.)
- SWIFT official publications
- NGO reports on financial exclusion and digital rights
- BibleGateway.com — Scriptural translations and cross-references

Appendix – Chapter 21 Sources

Scriptural References
- Galatians 5:20 — Pharmakeia as a work of the flesh
- Revelation 9:21 — Refusal to repent of sorceries
- Revelation 18:23 — Nations deceived by pharmakeia
- Genesis 3:1–5 — The serpent's deception in Eden
- Numbers 21:8–9 — The bronze serpent lifted by Moses (a symbol of healing through faith)

Ancient and Historical Sources
- Greek cult of Asclepius — Healing temples, serpent symbolism
- Hermes and the caduceus — Commerce, trickery, and boundaries
- Babylonian and Egyptian pharmakeia — Potions, incantations, and enchantments
- Medieval alchemy — Elixirs, transmutation, and proto-chemistry

Modern Pharmakeia
- Reports on opioid crisis and pharmaceutical dependency
- Studies on psychopharmacology and mood alteration
- Analyses of polypharmacy and chronic disease management
- Critiques of pharmaceutical monopolies and patents

Symbolism and Mythology
- Rod of Asclepius vs. Caduceus — Historical confusion and modern adoption
- Serpent symbolism in ancient religions
- Comparative mythology of healing and deception

Secondary Scholarship
- Michael Heiser, The Unseen Realm — Watchers and forbidden knowledge
- Mircea Eliade, The Forge and the Crucible — Alchemy and transformation
- Jacques Ellul, The Technological Society — Technology as control
- Richard Dolan, The Secret Space Program and Breakaway Civilization (for pharmakeia as control)

Online Resources
- WHO reports on pharmaceuticals and global health
- FDA archives on drug approvals and controversies
- Medical history resources on Asclepius and Hermes
- BibleGateway.com — Scriptural translations and cross-references

Appendix – Chapter 22 Sources

Scriptural References
- Genesis 3:1–5 — The serpent's deception

- Exodus 12:14 — Passover as remembrance
- Deuteronomy 6:12 — "Beware lest thou forget the LORD"
- Psalm 119:11 — Hiding the Word in the heart
- John 1:5 — The light shines in darkness
- John 14:26 — The Spirit brings remembrance
- Revelation 12:11 — Overcoming by the blood of the Lamb and the word of testimony
- Revelation 21:4 — GOD will wipe away every tear

Historical and Archaeological Witness
- Dead Sea Scrolls — Preservation of Scripture despite erasure
- Early Church Fathers — Testimonies of faith under persecution
- Archaeological inscriptions — Stones crying out when texts were silenced
- Oral traditions — Indigenous and biblical communities preserving memory

Comparative Mythology
- Trickster archetypes — Erasure through confusion
- Hero archetypes — Restoration through remembrance
- Flood myths — Memory preserved through survivors and archives

Secondary Scholarship
- Michael Heiser, The Unseen Realm — Divine council and remembrance
- Mircea Eliade, Myth and Reality — Memory as sacred continuity
- Jacques Ellul, The Technological Society — Erasure through modern systems
- N.T. Wright, The Resurrection of the Son of GOD — Memory and hope in Christ

Online Resources

- BibleGateway.com — Scriptural translations and cross-references
- Sefaria.org — Hebrew texts and commentaries
- Archaeology.org — Discoveries preserving biblical memory
- EarlyChristianWritings.com — Testimonies of early faith

About The Author

Drew Allen lives in East Tennessee with his wife of over 35 years and has three adult sons and (as of this writing) three grandchildren. Professionally, Drew is the founder of Atomic Cost LLC and is a seasoned consultant who has successfully served in management positions at many large and well-known companies for the nuclear, chemical process, and other industries around the world. His fraternal associations have included Master Mason of the Ancient Free and Accepted Masons (AF&AM), Order of the Knights Templar of the York Rite, Sublime Prince of the Royal Secret of the Ancient Scottish Rite, and Noble of the Ancient Arabic Order of the Nobles of the Mystic Shrine.

www.ingramcontent.com/pod-product-compliance
Lightning Source LLC
Chambersburg PA
CBHW050116280326
41933CB00010B/1129